THE PRINTED SQUARE

THE PRINTED SQUARE

Vintage Handkerchief Patterns for Fashion and Design

Nicky Albrechtsen

Thames & Hudson

with 240 illustrations, 234 in colour

CONTENTS

INTRODUCTION

For admirers and collectors, handkerchiefs are an abundant source of historical lacework, embroidery and embellishment. The early twentieth century was a particularly innovative and inspiring period of design, stimulated by the popularity of the printed handkerchief as an essential accessory. Unconstrained by prevailing fashions, fit and function, designers of handkerchiefs channelled all their energies into these small squares of fabric, displaying their unleashed creativity and obvious enjoyment through explosions of colour and pattern. The handkerchiefs in this book have been selected to reflect the magnificent array of printed designs between the 1920s and 1950s.

Color is the most important factor in design generally, and in handkerchief design specifically.
Tammis Keefe,
Craft Horizons, 1952

The handkerchief has played a vital role in the traditions of social etiquette throughout history. The Romans dropped a handkerchief known as a *mappa* to signal the start of the Circensian games, while their emperors carried handkerchiefs that were ornately embroidered and fringed with gold as a sign of prosperity and position. In the Middle Ages, jousting knights proclaimed a lady's favour by pinning her handkerchief or scarf to their sleeve. In the more recent past, the French military leader Napoleon Bonaparte is said to have carried his wife Joséphine's *mouchoir* whenever they were apart as a token of affection.

From pieces of linen found in Egyptian tombs to the functional 'napkins' and 'muck-minders' of the Renaissance era, the handkerchief gradually evolved from a utilitarian object into an ostentatious and elaborately decorated piece of cloth. In Europe, men and women carried a *couvrechef* – a French term meaning 'head cover', from which the English word *kerchief* derives – as a fashion accessory as early as the fifteenth century. Sprinkled with cologne, it was used coquettishly for flirtatious and romantic gestures: letting it drop to the ground, for example, was an invitation for friendship; twirling it in both hands indicated indifference; the gentle mopping of one's forehead was a sign of being watched; and drawing a handkerchief across one's cheek signified love.

Renaissance decoration took the form of simple drawn threadwork and delicate embroidery. In Tudor England ladies gave luxurious 'handkerchers' edged with handmade lace to their male admirers, who displayed them in their hats. Handkerchers were fashioned to match collars and cuffs in a wide variety of shapes and sizes, with elaborate decoration on both sides. These small fashion accessories were valued items and often documented in wedding trousseaus, wills and inventories. Henry VIII left fifteen dozen, embroidered in silver and gold, on his death in 1547.

Page 2:
A young woman creates a risqué outfit from her collection of handkerchiefs in this illustration from the early erotic magazine *La Vie Parisienne*, 7 October 1922.

Page 4:
This vibrant Art Deco handkerchief shows the richness and three-dimensional quality that was often achieved in patterns despite the limitations of early printing techniques.

Opposite, clockwise from top left:
Fred Astaire, c. 1930s; Cary Grant, late 1940s; Brigitte Bardot, c. 1960s.

In the seventeenth century, as the practice of snuff-taking grew in popularity among the aristocracy, handkerchiefs became not only more decorative but also more vibrant. The deep colours and ornate patterns of imported cottons from India and the Far East were ideal for so-called 'sneeze-catchers' (large oblong or oval handkerchiefs) since they masked the brown stains caused by snuff.

In the ostentatious royal court of late eighteenth-century France, fashions were famously elaborate and extravagant, setting the tone for the rest of Europe. On 2 June 1785 Louis XVI, encouraged by his wife Marie Antoinette, who had become tired of all the different shapes and sizes of handkerchief used by her courtiers, passed a law decreeing: 'The length of handkerchiefs shall equal their width throughout my entire kingdom.' Gradually the format of handkerchiefs was simplified: squares of varying sizes became standard, regardless of whether a handkerchief was intended as a fashion accessory or was purely functional.

With the practice of using engraved copperplates from 1770, and the introduction of the roller printer almost fifteen years later – both pioneered by Thomas Bell of Scotland – textile-printing processes became more advanced. The use of printing machines to apply colour to fabric improved both the efficiency of the process and the execution of the pattern, transforming textile production and design. Printed designs became a quick and inexpensive method of adding pattern to cloth. Handkerchiefs depicting famous portraits, maps, coach fares and timetables began to appear. Caricatures poking fun at politicians or notorious stories were particularly popular on men's handkerchiefs, while designs on children's hankies tended to be attractive, informative and educational – qualities that continued until the 1950s.

During the nineteenth century, handkerchiefs became somewhat more sophisticated in design. By the mid-century, English women of the upper and rapidly growing middle classes favoured elegantly embroidered white handkerchiefs, often monogrammed and edged with machine-made lace, while a gentleman was rarely seen without a plain dark or white handkerchief in his breast pocket, echoing the sombre fashions of the Victorian era. With the death of a loved one, all members of the household were subject to the strict rules of mourning, which required a woman to remain in full mourning – to dress entirely in black and wear a veil – for one year and a day on the passing of her husband.

These restrictions extended to the type of accessory she used, including handkerchiefs, which were either black or white edged in black embroidery. Queen Victoria had many mourning handkerchiefs made following the death of her beloved husband, Albert, in 1861, and popularized their use.

The great advancements in manufacturing, production and industrial design that marked the early decades of the twentieth century earned this era the name of the 'machine age'. Form and function heavily influenced design and pattern, which concentrated on surface decoration rather than the intricate craftsmanship of the Victorian era and the Arts and Crafts movement. The fusion of artistic influences that embraced the flowing lines of Art Nouveau and the abstraction of Art Deco, and referenced art from Japan, Egypt and Central America (specifically the Aztecs) resulted in a diversity of textile design that had never been experienced before. Every taste could be indulged from the variety of patterns on offer, and handkerchiefs were no exception.

Upper-class women often carried two handkerchiefs: one for use, which remained hidden, the other for show. By the 1920s, these 'dress' handkerchiefs were frequently made of expensive fabrics such as chiffon or silk. Wealthy women had a handkerchief for every occasion: plain and simple for the morning; printed and decorative for afternoon tea; and extravagant for dinners, theatre outings and balls. There were special handkerchiefs for sports such as tennis, horse riding and golf, and a particular favourite might be saved for Sunday best.

A humorous article in *Vogue* magazine, published in July 1922, touches on the importance that was attached to this diminutive fashion accessory in the Roaring Twenties: 'Handkerchiefs and reputations are exceedingly easy to lose. Both are lost in about equal numbers daily. All the reputations lost are very good ones – and the more irretrievably lost they are, the better they were. The handkerchiefs lost should be better. Imagine a lady saying, "My reputation is gone, but I

A powder-puff handkerchief, c. 1920. Usually made from silk chiffon, the powder puff came into use at the turn of the twentieth century.

don't care. It wasn't any good." Yet that is exactly the attitude she takes toward a lost handkerchief.'

Some of the powder-puff handkerchiefs of the 1920s and 1930s were particularly exquisite. An earlier article in the *New York Times* (1911) concerning a ruling on customs duties for imported goods provides a detailed description: 'The merchandise consisted of hemstitched silk handkerchiefs about nine inches square. In the centre a circular piece of silk is applied by a double row of stitching through which runs a draw cord or string. To the circular piece of silk is attached a disc of down which is intended to be used as a powder puff. After using the puff the down may be concealed from view by the use of the draw cord.'

Forerunners of the modern compact, these powder-puff handkerchiefs were manufactured in industrial cities such as Bradford, Huddersfield, Manchester and Macclesfield in northern England, at a time when the United States imported the majority of its printed textiles. (Macclesfield was one of the main producers of handkerchiefs between the 1920s and 1940s and now houses a museum with an extensive archive of printed designs.) The ruling cited in the article centred on whether the item was classified as a handkerchief or a powder puff: handkerchiefs were liable for import tax, while the powder puff was exempt. Although these luxury items are described as having had a drawstring, most of the examples that survive today have none: the handkerchief was simply folded over the puff to stop the powder from spilling over the contents of a handbag.

With the technological advancements of the 1920s and 1930s came the golden age of Hollywood. Dressed by leading couturiers, the stars of the silver screen were idolized by fans who imitated their style and fashions. Screen sirens such as Marlene Dietrich,

Greta Garbo and Katharine Hepburn were the embodiment of Hollywood glamour in outfits by celebrated designers such as Madeleine Vionnet, famed for her sensual bias-cut and chiffon dresses featuring her signature handkerchief hemline. Home sewing was a common pastime and, although handkerchiefs tended to be relatively inexpensive to buy, many women made their own to complement particular outfits. Style icon Dietrich led the way, exhibiting a soft chiffon handkerchief in the breast pocket of a tailored jacket. She is said to have had small squares of chiffon stitched into her pockets to add sex appeal to the masculine-style clothing that she favoured.

Mail order provided an essential service for many families living in an age when travel was expensive and inadequate. Many department stores, especially in the United States, produced catalogues that were lavishly illustrated, with whole pages devoted to the intricate handkerchief patterns available. The American catalogue *Bellas Hess* had particularly beautiful illustrations, often featuring handkerchiefs with the bold, daring geometric designs of the Art Deco movement advocated by fashion designers such as Jeanne Lanvin, Sonia Delaunay and Paul Poiret.

In 1924 the American company Kimberly-Clark launched Kleenex disposable tissues, originally marketed as a wipe for cold cream and make-up removal. Endorsed by Hollywood film stars, they caught on very quickly. The introduction of pretty pastel colours and a shift in advertising strategy a few years later encouraged the practice of using a Kleenex tissue as a disposable handkerchief.

The paper restrictions of the Second World War limited the manufacture of Kleenex for this purpose, so this disposable handkerchief was used instead as a sterile dressing for wounds. Traditional handkerchiefs, on the other hand, became popular gifts during this period of austerity and sometimes carried messages of endearment. It was not uncommon for soldiers serving abroad to send handkerchiefs embroidered with romantic messages to their sweethearts back home. Other messages were politically motivated: in England, where two handkerchiefs could be purchased with one ration coupon, handkerchiefs were issued based on designs for propaganda posters.

Post-war design in general moved away from the exploration of decadent and elaborate style and decoration. The aftermath of the Second World War brought a need for realism and functionality with sympathetically streamlined aesthetics in all genres of design. However, handkerchiefs continued to be sought after as small, personal expressions of style and sustained their appeal, owing in part to the array of attractive designs and colours available. Modern manufacturing and printing processes allowed

for endless variations in design. The striking red Lipstick handkerchief, ideal for blotting the pillarbox red made fashionable by film icons, was a mainstay of many a handbag in the 1950s. Again, a star of the screen, Joan Crawford, is said to have been the inspiration for the Lipstick handkerchief. While dining out in a Hollywood restaurant with a film producer, she was reportedly mortified by the scarlet smears left on her white handkerchief and duly ordered red ones from her dressmaker.

While women would rarely go out without a handkerchief in their bags, men wore theirs openly: a man in a suit would not dream of being seen in public without a pocket square tucked into his jacket. There were numerous types of fold to choose from, from the 'presidential' (with the square folded at right angles to fit the pocket) to the 'puff' (which, as the name suggests, is loosely folded to create a rounded shape).

Department stores devoted whole sections to the sale of traditional handkerchiefs, adorned with floral prints, souvenirs, commemorative items, animals, film stars and cartoons. Two American manufacturers, Burmel and Kimball, regularly competed for advertising space in *Vogue* and promoted their latest designs through campaigns such as 'Handkerchief of the Month' and 'Flower of the Month' respectively. The post-war

Above left:
Marlene Dietrich.

Above right:
Joan Crawford,
Buenos Aires,
Argentina, 1960.

handkerchief was transformed into a commercial product. There were handkerchiefs for special occasions, including Mother's Day, Easter and Christmas. Others were used as an advertising tool to promote holiday destinations and cultural events. The 1951 Festival of Britain, both the 1939 and 1964 New York World's Fairs, and the coronations of Edward VIII and Elizabeth II were all commemorated on handkerchiefs.

The mid-1950s witnessed an advertising boom that fuelled a burgeoning consumerism. Seductive images encouraging the purchase of particular products were projected through the new media of television, glossy magazines and giant billboards. American consumers were introduced to 'Little Lulu and Her Magic Tricks', an undisguised advertising ploy: disposable Kleenex tissues were sold attached to a book in which Lulu instructed children in the art of performing magic tricks with tissues. Little Lulu's smiling cartoon face typified the new mood of 1950s graphic design, characterized by happy, friendly animations designed to inspire confidence in the consumer – a style that influenced the increasingly commercial floral and geometric textile designs of 1950s fabric handkerchiefs.

However, by the late 1950s, sales of traditional handkerchiefs had begun to dwindle, driven by public health campaigns advocating the use of disposable tissues. Kleenex, meanwhile, perhaps buoyed by the short-lived fashion in the 1960s for paper dresses and disposable underwear, continued to flourish. As the new disposable culture prevailed, handkerchiefs gradually returned to being viewed as purely functional objects, no longer enjoyed for their design and decoration.

Although the fabric handkerchief has widely lost its status, some traditional associations have survived. In Japanese culture the cotton handkerchief known as a *tenugui*, printed in an assortment of designs, is a common gift between acquaintances; as in days gone by, it is used for mopping heads and wiping hands rather than blowing noses. Meanwhile, in many countries of the western world, a handkerchief remains a traditional accessory for a man in a tailored suit. In the words of American menswear designer and author Alan Flusser, 'Leaving a breast pocket unattended is like trying to spell "classic" without the "class".'

DESIGNS OF
THE DECADES

Printed handkerchiefs are a rich but largely neglected source of pattern and colour. In the early twentieth century a handkerchief was chosen purely for its charm; there were no designer labels or sales gimmicks to influence prospective purchasers. A textile designer required great imagination and skill to create a hand-kerchief that responded to the fashions of the period yet made a bold statement. Dating from the 1920s onwards, the handkerchiefs in this book display exceptional decoration and technique, creative colour combinations, and a lively mix of geometric and floral elements. Individually, they are beautiful examples of twentieth-century prints; collectively, they reveal original approaches to design that are truly inspirational.

Cloth is one of the most beautiful and vibrant things in the world… Anything is possible in textile design, if it is done correctly. A designer merely starts with something, anything, and then develops it. Tammis Keefe, *Christian Science Monitor*, 1951

Printed handkerchiefs from the turn of the twentieth century are rare. Designs bearing the fluid, curvilinear forms of Art Nouveau are particularly scarce. Most surviving examples from this era are embroidered or feature elaborate monograms. As handkerchiefs were seldom signed by designers, it is also difficult to study the work of an individual artist. Notable exceptions are Scottish artist and architect Charles Rennie Mackintosh and his wife Margaret MacDonald, who were leading exponents of the Arts and Crafts movement and designed textiles for several companies, including Liberty, during the latter part of their careers. Among these were beautiful designs for handkerchiefs, which now form part of the collections of the Victoria & Albert Museum in London and the Hunterian Museum and Art Gallery in Glasgow, although it is not known whether these designs were ever put into production.

Following the Great War, the curved, naturalistic forms of Art Nouveau gradually gave way to the precise, geometric lines of Art Deco. Reaching its peak in the 1920s, Art Deco drew on a range of influences, from Cubism, Russian Constructivism and Italian Futurism to the growing impact of the machine and aerodynamic design on everyday life. Many handkerchiefs from this era feature a striking combination of regular lines and shapes, including squares, triangles, stripes and zigzags. The men's handkerchiefs in particular often have a three-dimensional quality, achieved using only two colours and characterized by dramatic contrasts of red and blue, orange and brown, or black and white. Many women's handkerchiefs were handmade from scraps of silk dresses and blouses and were decorated with large-scale, stylized flowers and bold geometric

Handkerchiefs of the 1920s were often made by hand from the offcut of a chiffon dress or blouse, as shown in this example.

shapes in the pastel shades (dusty pinks, cool blues and earthy browns) that were fashionable at the time. During the 1920s and 1930s there was a trend for the shape of a handkerchief to follow the outline of the design rather than the standard square format.

During the 1920s handkerchief-shaped godets – pieces of material inserted in a garment to make it flared or for ornamentation – were often used in skirts and dresses of layered chiffon, creating the uneven, choppy handkerchief hemline. This was a popular style for evening dresses as it allowed women to move freely when dancing the Charleston, and it remained in style well into the 1930s. Similarly, the handkerchief sleeve was a feature of many 1920s evening dresses. Usually short or three-quarter length, this sleeve fell into graceful points like the corners of a handkerchief, a style that re-emerged in the maxi dresses and smocks of the 1970s. The trend even extended to furniture with the so-called handkerchief table, which featured a triangular top and drop-down leaves that resembled a gentlemen's folded pocket square. Originally designed in the eighteenth century and primarily used as a card table, this corner piece enjoyed renewed popularity in the 1920s.

With advances in printing techniques and improvements in the colourfastness of dyes in the 1930s came a more detailed approach to textile design. Bold geometric forms and polka dots complemented colourful floral motifs, which in turn became highly intricate. Handkerchiefs displayed striking colour combinations such as lilac, peach and green, or yellow, blue and orange. The use of green dyes on textiles produced mixed results, with the colour often fading too quickly, and printed fabrics of this era frequently feature floral motifs with grey or yellow leaves. 'Grinning', a term that refers to the halo effect of off-register printing, is another characteristic of 1930s textiles. This technique, whereby areas of the light ground show through a printed area of fabric owing to the different elements of a pattern not aligning precisely, was developed to prevent the accidental overlap of colours. Thus the floral and geometric motifs that dominated handkerchief designs of this period regularly appeared to have a thin white border, which broke up the blocks of colour and became an integral part of the design.

Towards the end of the decade women's handkerchiefs often featured borders of contrasting patterns. The use of alternating bands of floral and geometric motifs, creating a broad and ornate border, was particularly effective. These designs are reminiscent of the folk prints of the 1970s yet also have a timeless quality. Corners were also considered in the overall design and were typically decorated with posies and twirling ribbons. At the same time, Art Deco remained influential. The smooth-edged geometric forms that were a key element of this style lent themselves well to interesting formations within the confines of a small square.

The Second World War impacted both handkerchief production and design, particularly in Europe. Silk and dyes were in short supply as they were needed for essential equipment such as parachutes and uniforms. Supplies of the synthetic dyes used to print handkerchiefs were especially limited as they had been imported from Germany before the war. The delicate floral prints from the early 1940s are regularly found with blue leaves as green dyes were required for uniforms. Colour palettes, although often subdued, were used to give a bright accent to the austere utility clothing of the period. In England, patriotic designs in red, white and blue as well as propaganda prints were worn with pride. Rayon, a fabric made from regenerated cellulose that is absorbent and takes printed colour well, became the wartime substitute for silk. Motifs tended to be small. Ribbons intertwined with climbing plants were popular elements, inspired by antique designs. Another notable characteristic of some handkerchiefs is a textured, brushstroke-like effect in the field, which gives an irregularity to the overall print.

The relatively modest handkerchiefs of the 1940s were gradually replaced by lively, bold designs featuring large-scale floral motifs and fun graphic elements. In the years immediately following the war, fabric remained in limited supply, and leading manufacturers and designers continued to search for an alternative to silk. Many handkerchiefs of the early 1950s were made of parachute silk, which was available in abundance after the war, and nylon, a fashionable new fabric that took colour well. Nylon was a particularly popular choice for dress handkerchiefs, but it proved less functional. Cotton, which had previously been seen as functional rather than fashionable owing to its widespread use by the working class, began to appear in the collections of Christian Dior, Balmain, Jacques Fath and Jean Dessès and was advocated by leading textile manufacturers such as Zika Ascher. As a quote from the British paper *The Daily Telegraph* (1949) highlights, 'Cotton, which for so many years in the fashion world has been regarded as the country cousin to silk, has suddenly come to town.' The cotton handkerchiefs of

A typical 1940s floral print. Made of rayon, this handkerchief features small, interconnected floral motifs and an irregular, textured effect in the field.

A conversational piece by the prolific American textile designer Tammis Keefe, showing her artistic use of everyday objects as whimsical motifs.

the 1950s were unashamedly bright and floral, a print style that was popularized by Schiaparelli, Dior and Ascher.

In the United States, several textile designers emerged who specialized almost exclusively in handkerchiefs. Their signatures were displayed on their designs, and many adopted the conversational or novelty style of print that became so fashionable. Among the most prolific was Tammis Keefe, who occasionally worked under the name Peg Thomas and also designed household linens and scarves. Discussing her work in *American Fabrics* magazine (1948), she explained her approach of treating everyday 'current objects…artistically'. Her designs for handkerchiefs tended to be detailed, observational and yet naive in style, characterized by repeated whimsical motifs in soft colour blends. Other notable American designers who signed their handkerchiefs were Billie Kompa, Vera, Faith Austin, Pat Prichard and Jeanne Miller. They all had a strong figurative and commercial style that crossed over into the home furnishings market, with their designs appearing on an array of different items, from tea towels and napkins to oven gloves.

The influence of the handkerchief also extended to glassware. In 1948 Italian designer Paolo Venini, in collaboration with Fulvio Bianconi, perfected the technique of moulding a sheet of glass over a block so that it hung in folds. Known as the *fazzoletto* ('handkerchief') vase, once turned upside down it resembled a handkerchief with the corners and sides pulled upwards. Widely copied, the vase was displayed on many sideboards in the 1950s and often featured decorative glass that drew inspiration from handkerchief patterns, including details such as spots and stripes.

The 1950s were the most productive decade in the history of handkerchief design. The hope and optimism of the post-war years were conveyed in bright, exuberant prints. Travel, leisure and hobbies became popular themes, with handkerchiefs sporting cartoon characters, Hollywood stars and exotic holiday destinations. Innovative novelty prints, although sometimes viewed as kitsch by modern standards, represented an exciting new direction in fabric design. Floral patterns were particularly fashionable, with designers creating a profusion of prints that exploded with colour, from energetic shades of red, turquoise and yellow to striking combinations of salmon pink and black. The prints of roses and single-stem rosebuds are among the most iconic handkerchief designs of this era. Expanding on the theme of nature, some designers also introduced birds into their prints. Not content with simply expanding their themes and sources of inspiration, designers experimented with the handkerchief shape, often following the outline of the pattern in a similar way to designs of the 1920s and 1930s. These non-square designs were especially popular in the United States, where round, frilly and scalloped handkerchiefs were among the many available variations.

Meanwhile, the wider fashion for artist-designed prints seemed to have had little impact on handkerchiefs. Notable figures such as Henry Moore, Cecil Beaton, Feliks Topolski and Henri Matisse issued textile designs that catered to the 1950s fashion for bright geometrics, whimsical figuratives, painterly abstraction and atomic prints. One American painter, Carl Tait, designed prints specifically for handkerchiefs. His strong designs, often executed in a soft colour palette, bear testament to his background as a skilled graphic designer and illustrator.

film star

gary cooper

Opposite:
A handkerchief depicting Gary Cooper, 1950s. Hollywood had a particularly big influence on fashion during this era. Handkerchiefs were perfect-sized mementos of favourite films such as the Western *High Noon* (1952), for which Cooper won an Academy Award.

Above left:
Robert Redford takes the lead in the film adaptation of *The Great Gatsby*, 1974. The classic novel by F. Scott Fitzgerald (1925), on which the film is based, has become synonymous with the decadence of the early 1920s.

Below left:
Maureen O'Sullivan and William Powell star in *The Thin Man*, 1934, based on the detective novel of the same year by Dashiell Hammett. Powell wears his handkerchief in the shape known as the 'puff'.

ELEGANCIAS

Agosto, 1924

Left:
This August 1924
Elegancias magazine
cover depicts a young
girl gesturing with
her handkerchief.
Handkerchiefs
were used to signal
romantic messages,
especially during
the Victorian era.

Opposite above:
The *fazzoletto*
('handkerchief') vase,
originally designed in
1948 by Paolo Venini
and Fulvio Bianconi,
was a feature of many
1950s sideboards.

Opposite below:
The Handkerchief
Chair, designed in
1985 by Massimo and
Lella Vignelli, was
inspired by the light,
soft contours of a
handkerchief floating
through the air.

By the end of the decade, the traditional handkerchief had reached its peak. Advances in textile technology following the war had resulted in new synthetic fabrics with easy-care qualities, which gave designers greater scope to respond to consumer needs and demands. The emphasis on leisure that originated in the United States soon took hold in Europe, with the introduction of casual and sportswear for men and women. Women in particular had new working opportunities accompanied by increasing time pressures. As the strict rules of dress etiquette began to disappear, the traditional handkerchief slowly gave way to the disposable tissue.

The designer handkerchief is a much later arrival. As with vintage scarves, it is extremely difficult to pinpoint precisely when couture houses began to promote their names on these accessories. In the latter half of the twentieth century, Hermès, Ceil Chapman, Nina Ricci, Lanvin, Christian Dior, Hanae Mori, Vivienne Westwood and Zandra Rhodes, among others, all put their name to handkerchiefs. However, the designer handkerchief remains essentially a component of the male wardrobe, fuelled by the consumerism of the 1980s.

Although its popularity has declined over the past fifty years, the printed handkerchief has left a lasting legacy in the field of textile design. With the enormous range of motifs and colours as well as variations in shape and material, the handkerchief was a highly versatile fashion accessory. Its impact continues to be felt, not only in fashion but also in other areas of design such as furniture. One of the best examples of its adaptive nature is the so-called Handkerchief Chair, designed in 1985 by Massimo and Lella Vignelli. Taking the light, soft contours of the pocket square as its inspiration, it bears witness to the enduring appeal of the handkerchief throughout history as an effortlessly elegant yet functional object.

Of all the hues, reds have
the most potency.

JACK LENOR LARSEN

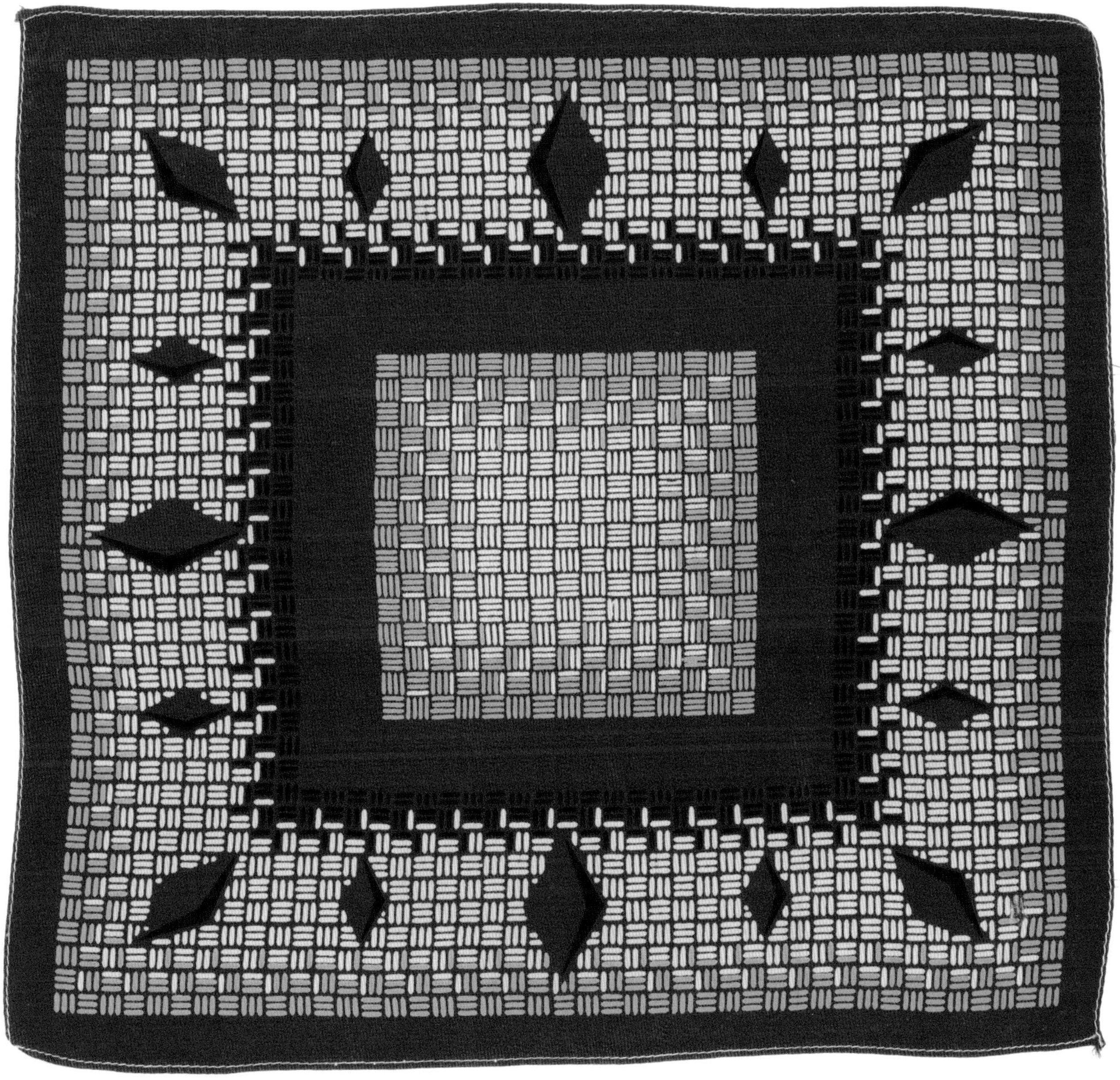

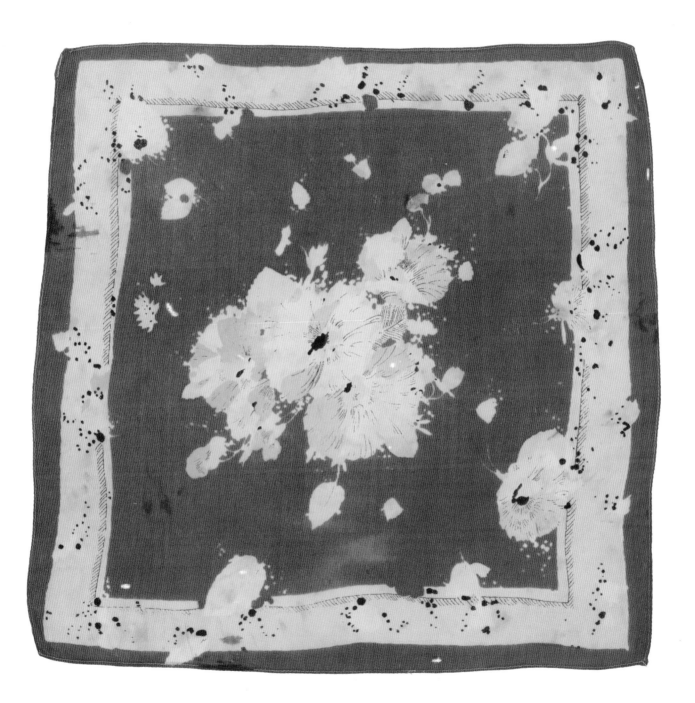

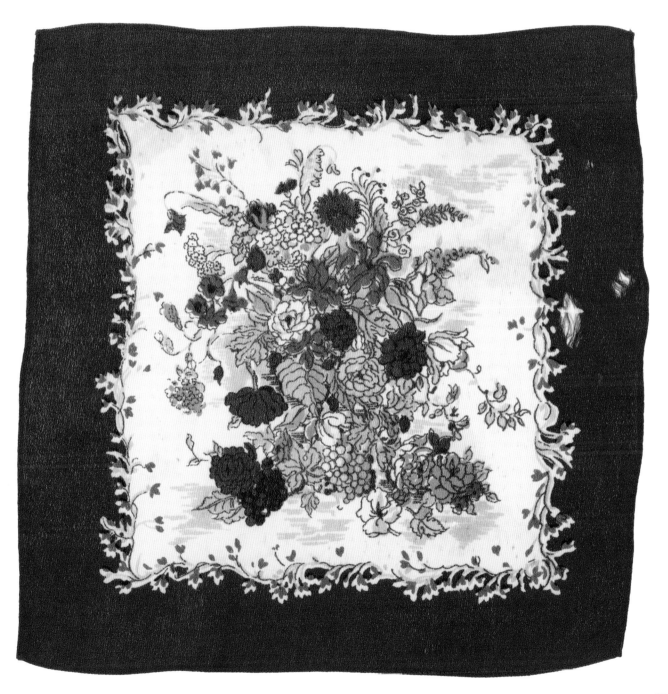

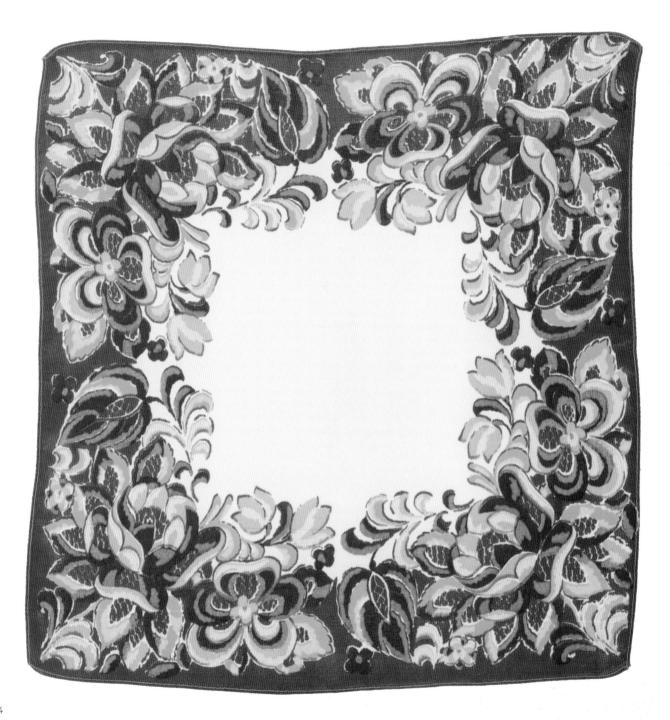

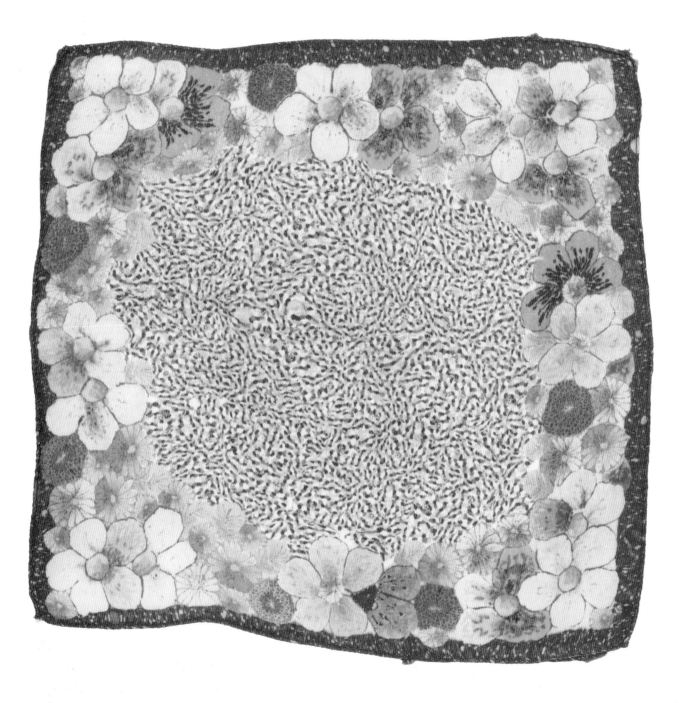

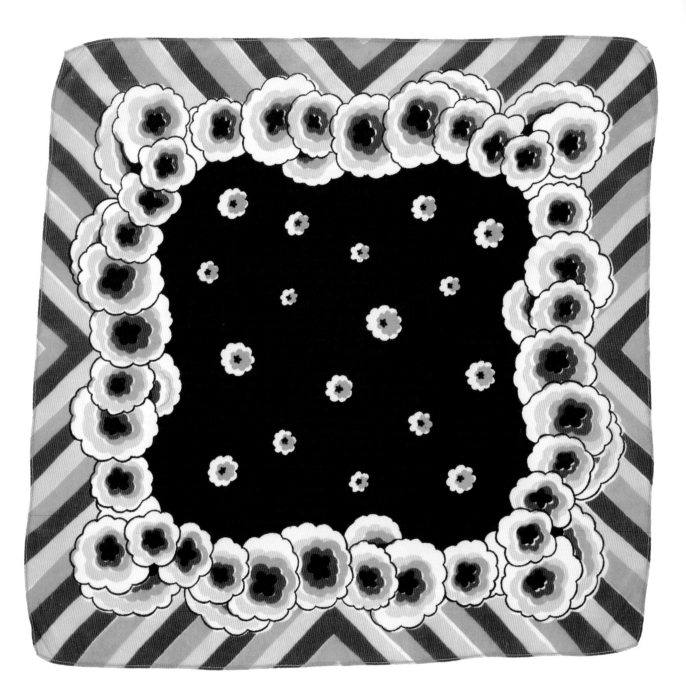

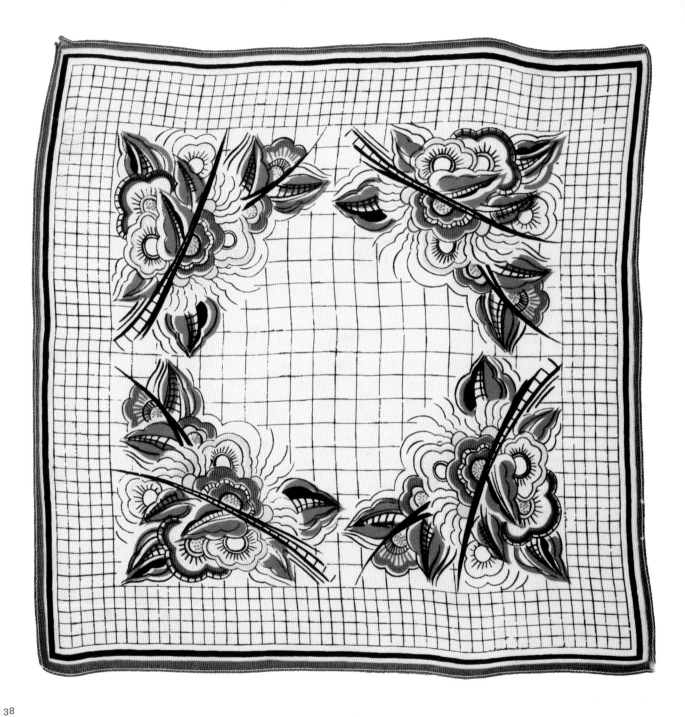

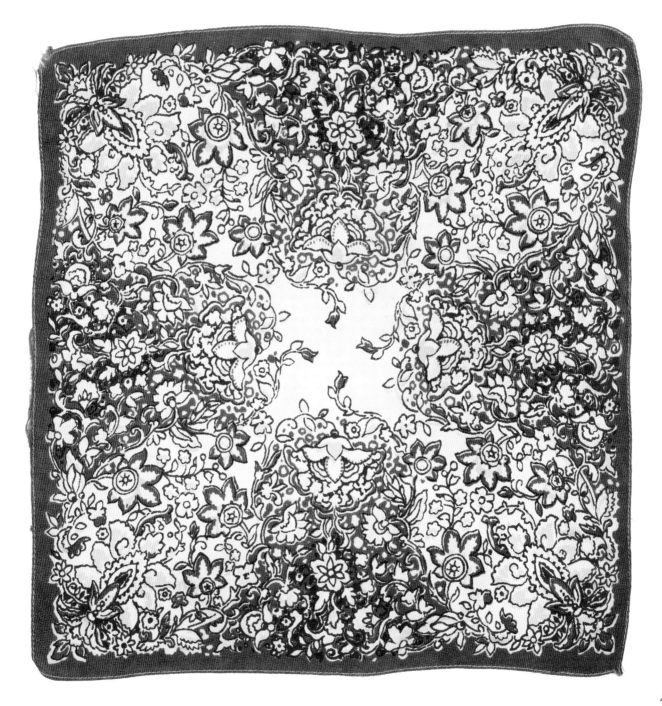

45

Orange is red brought
nearer to humanity
by yellow.

WASSILY KANDINSKY

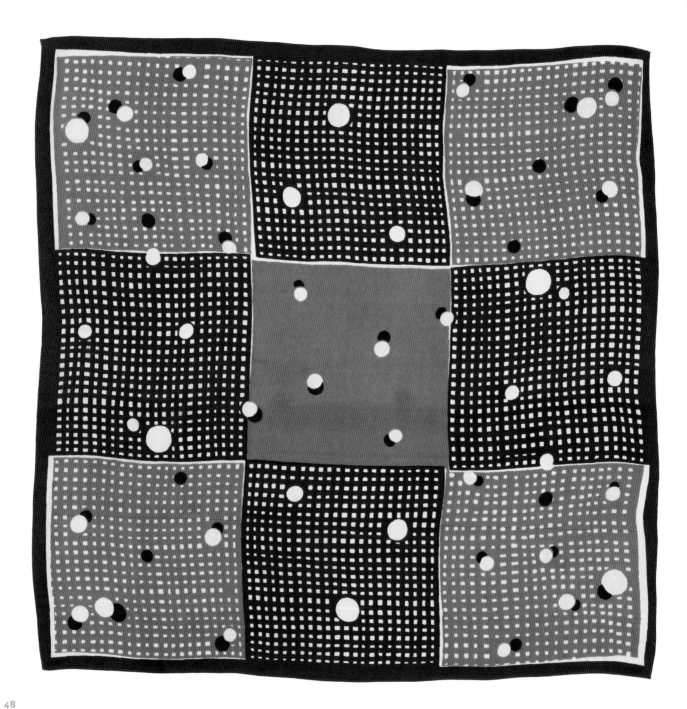

51

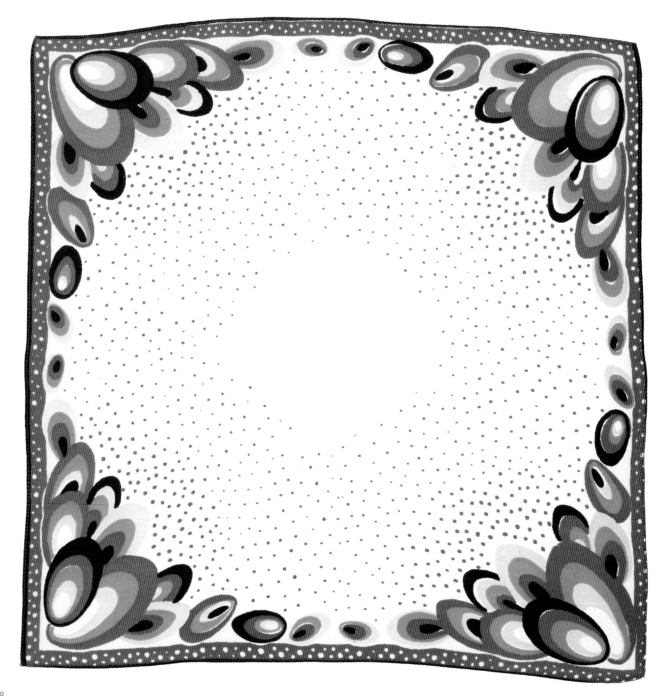

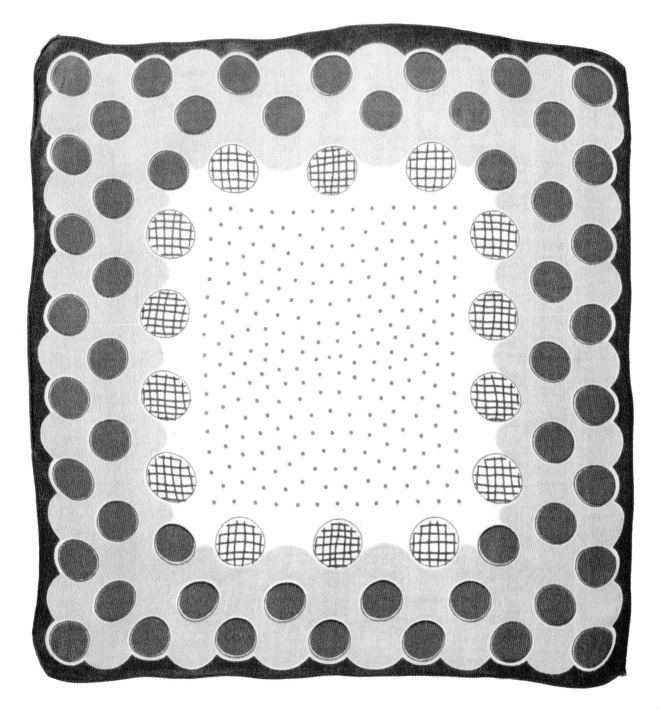

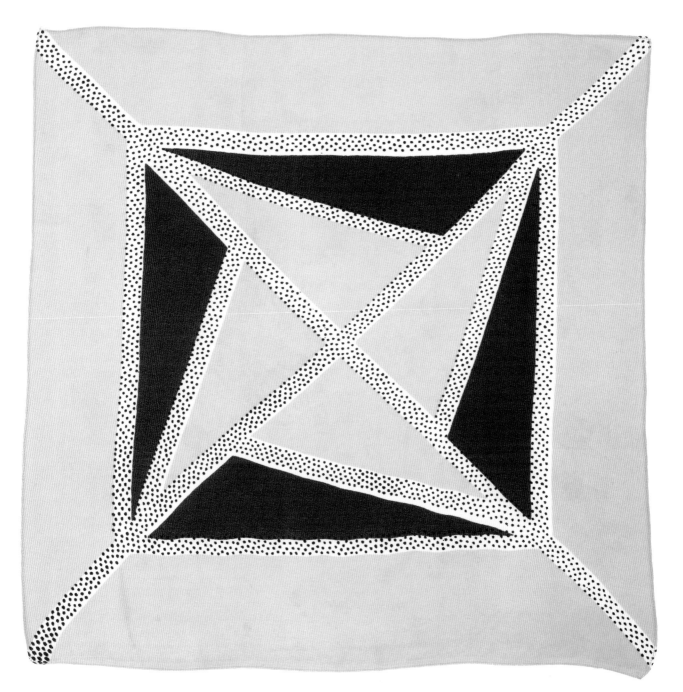

61

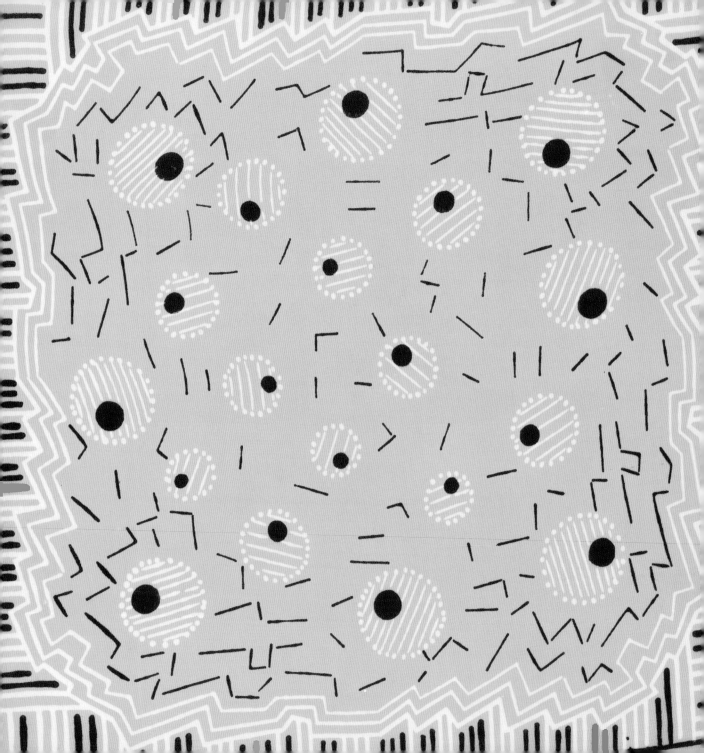

How lovely yellow is!
It stands for the sun.

VINCENT VAN GOGH

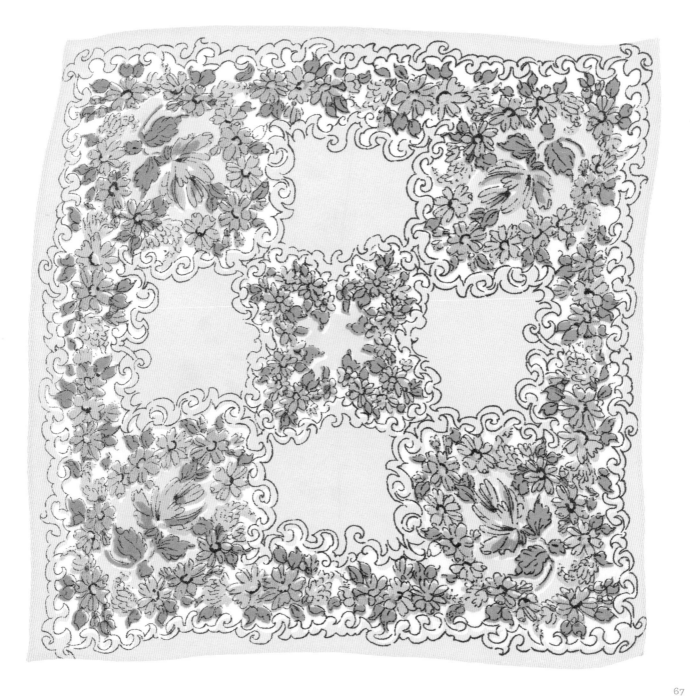

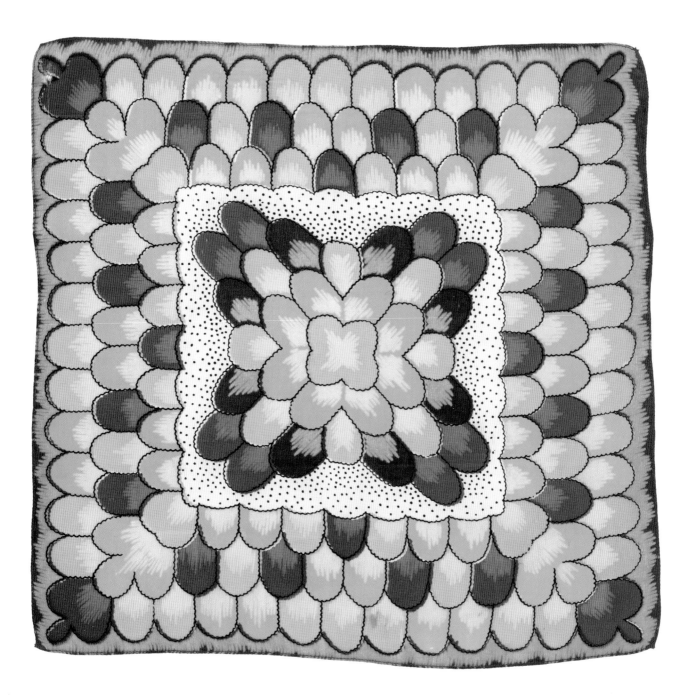

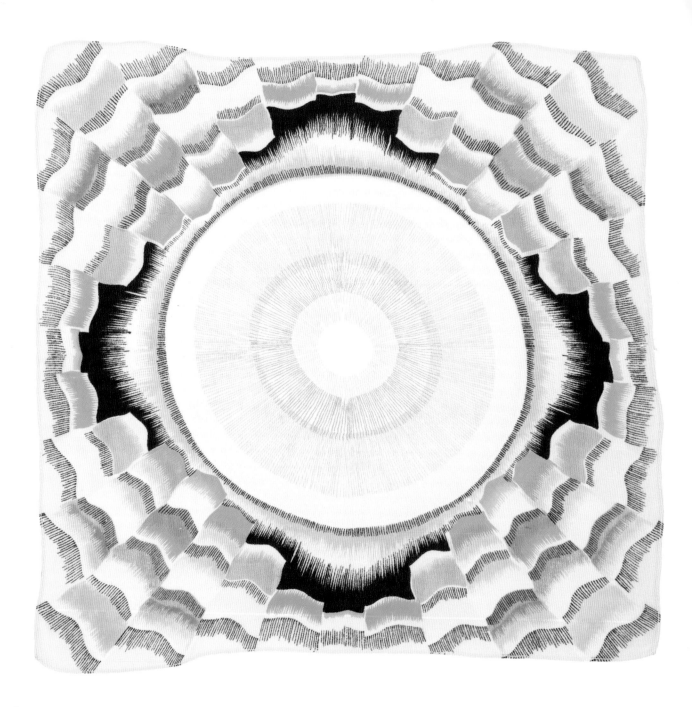

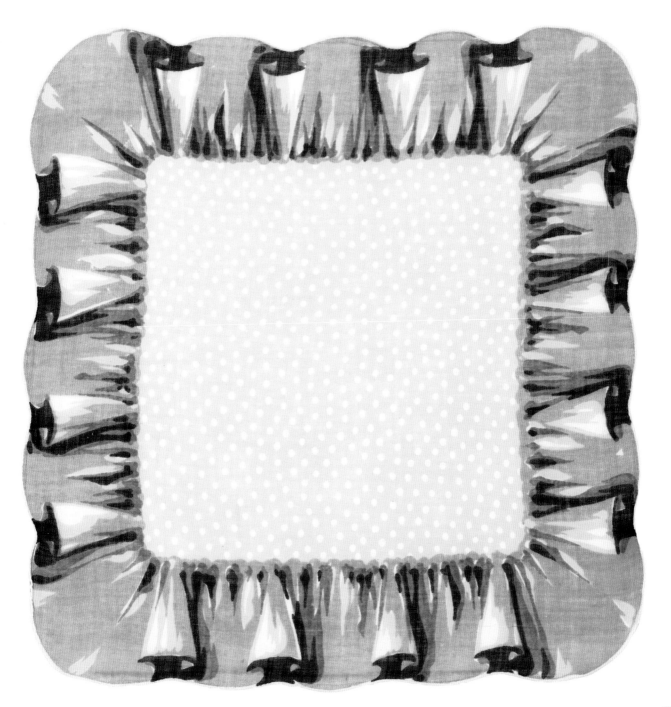

Green is the prime colour
of the world, and that from
which its loveliness arises.

PEDRO CALDERÓN DE LA BARCA

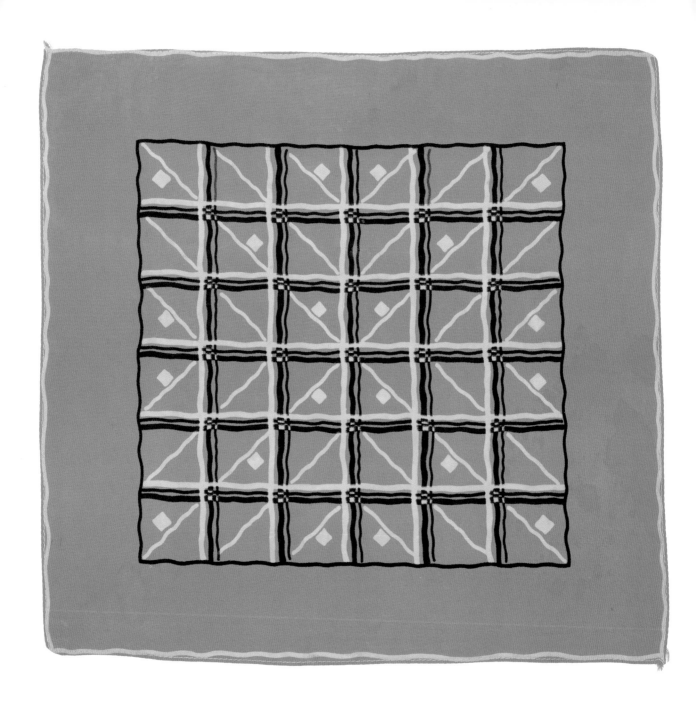

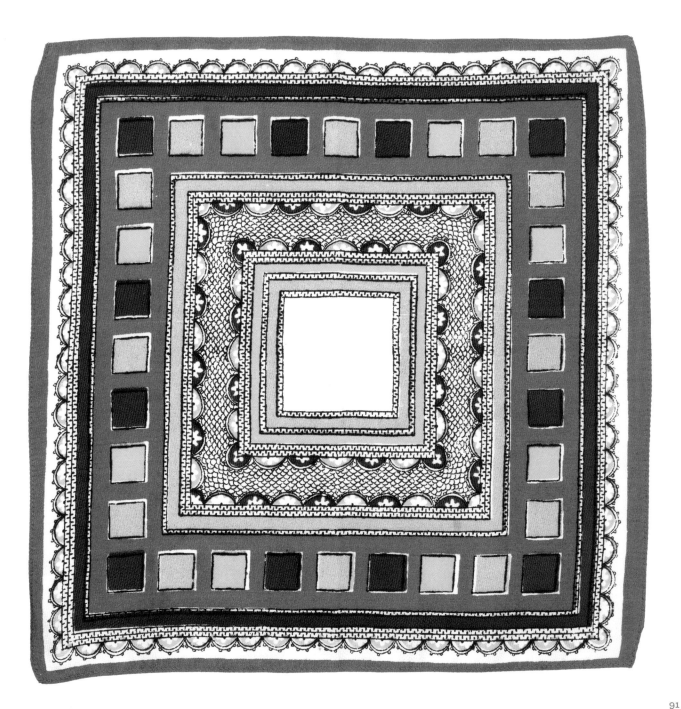

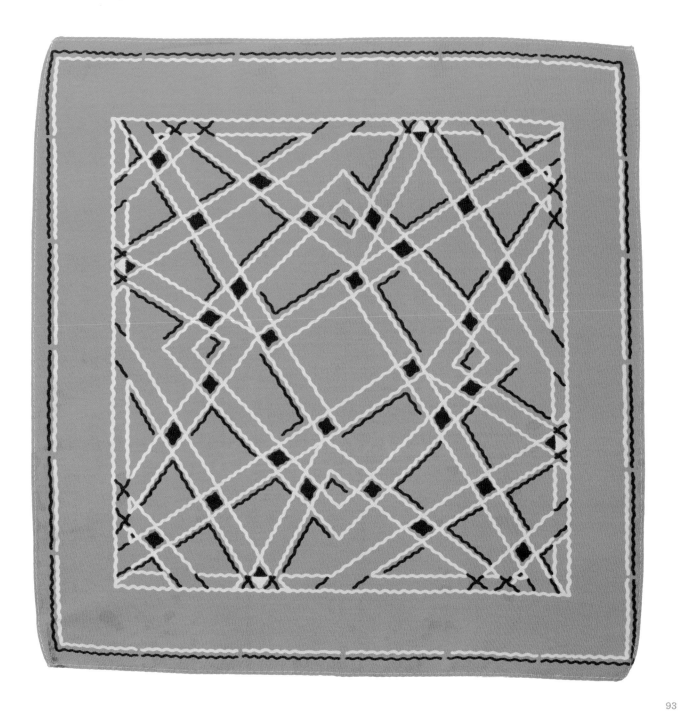

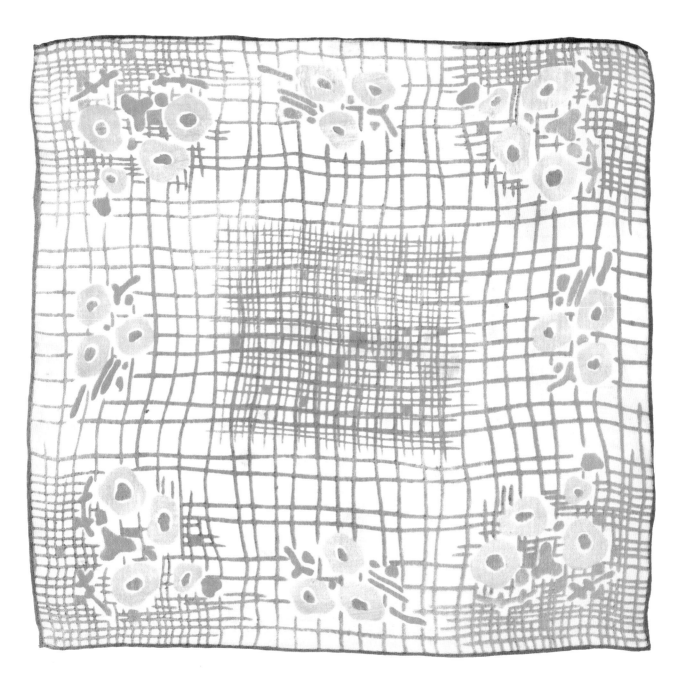

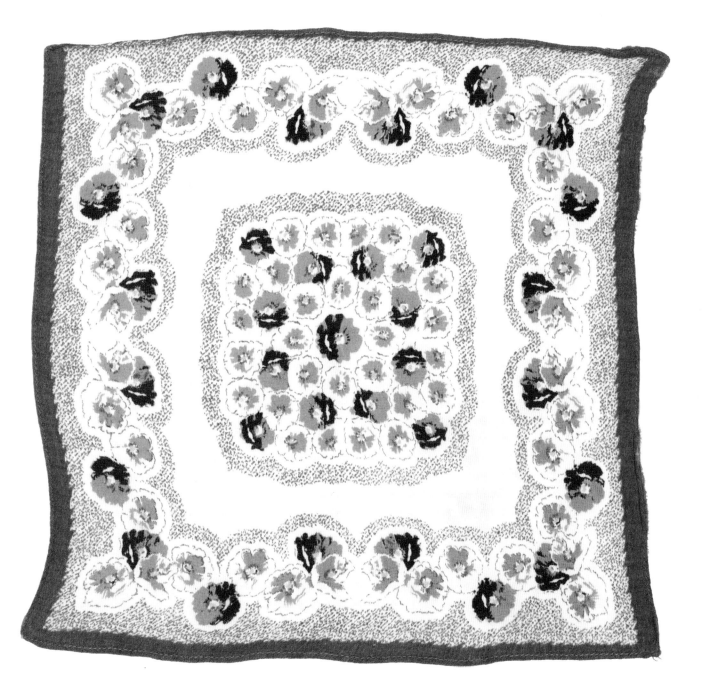

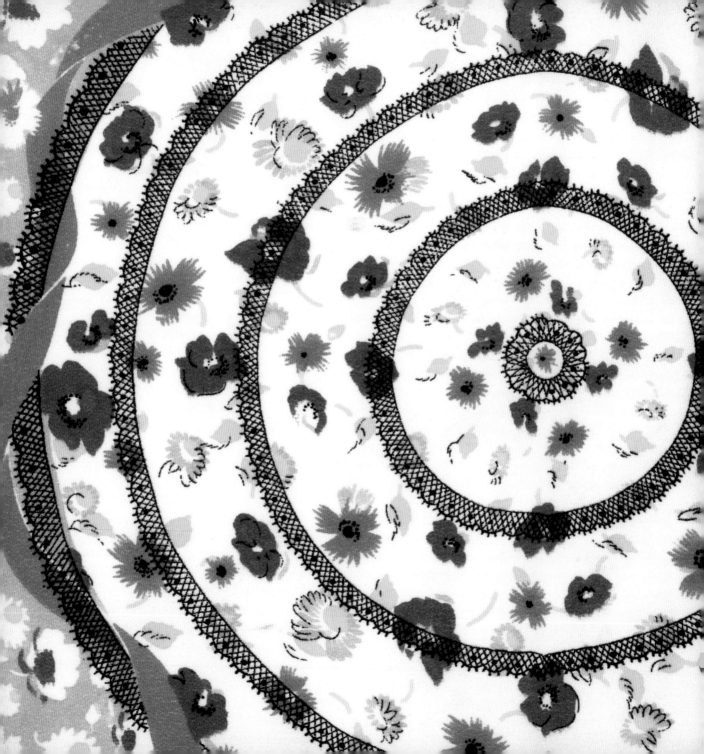

More varied than any landscape was the landscape in the sky, with islands of gold and silver, peninsulas of apricot and rose against a background of many shades of turquoise and azure.

CECIL BEATON

103

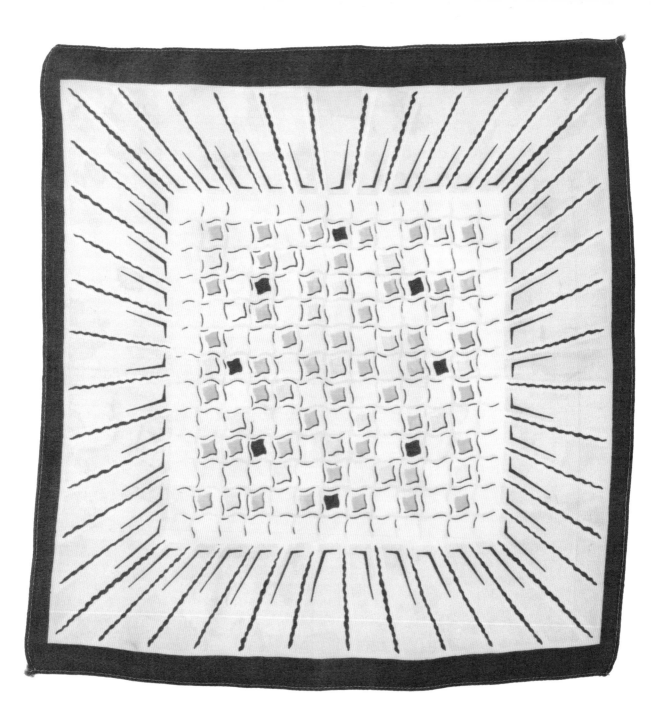

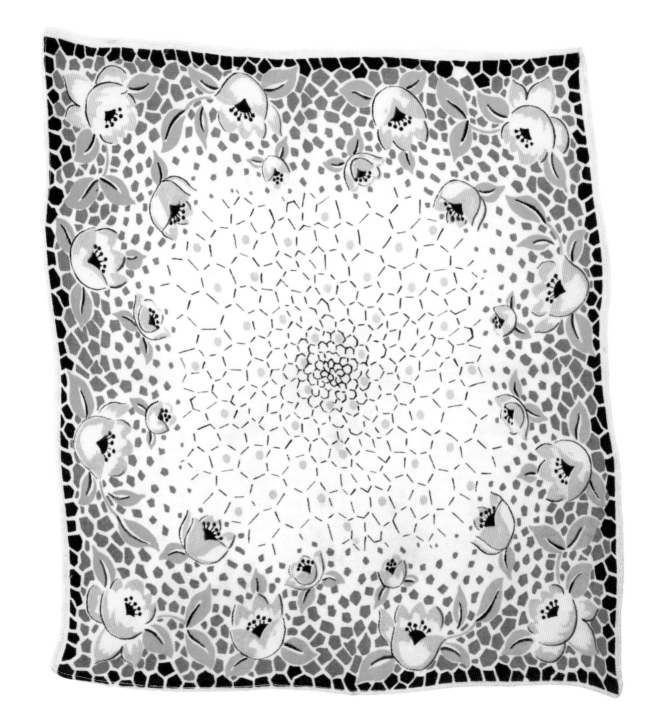

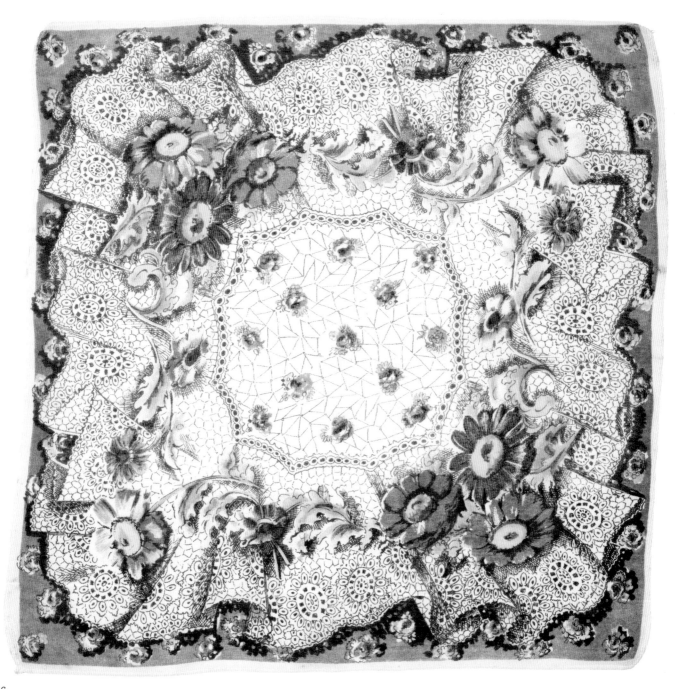

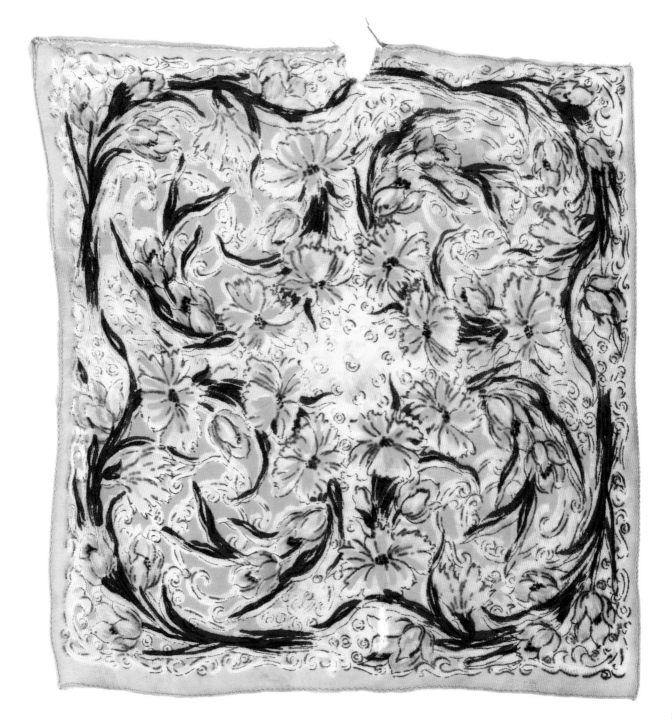

111

117

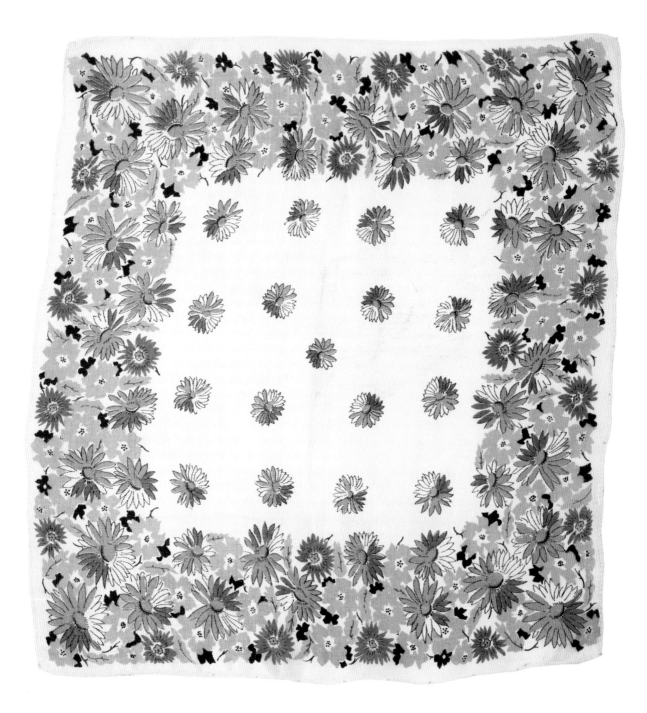

Blue colour is everlastingly
appointed by the deity to
be a source of delight.

JOHN RUSKIN

129

131

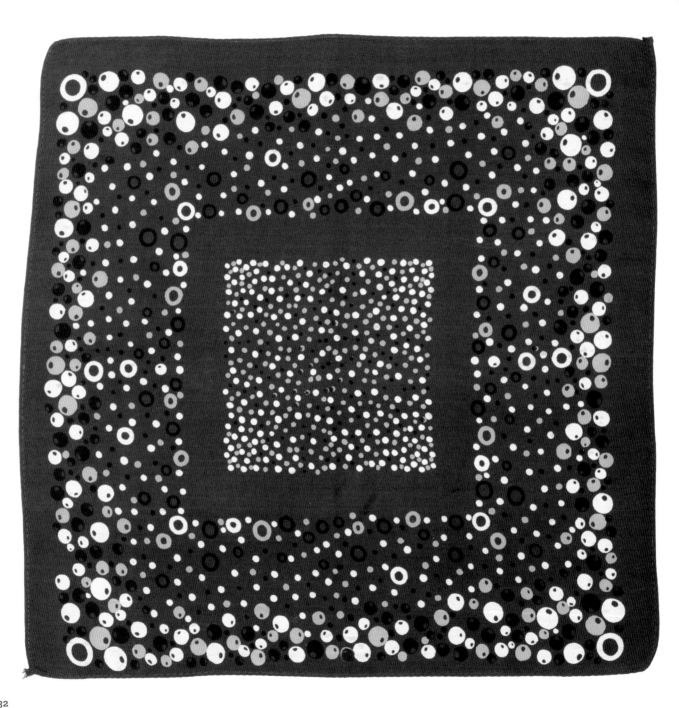

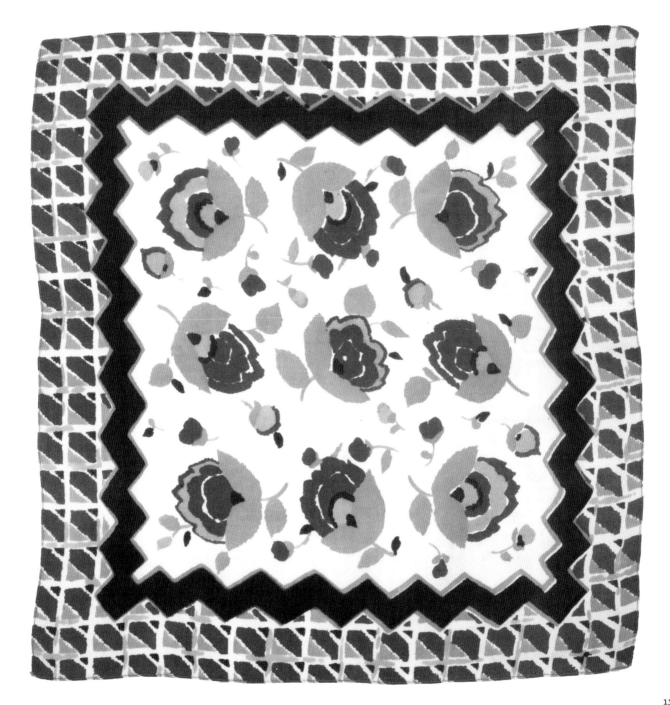

137

139

141

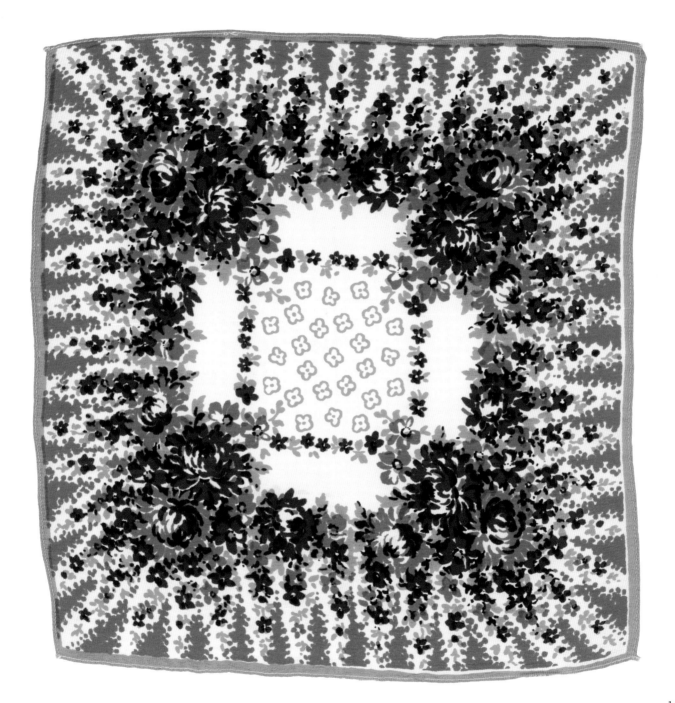

144

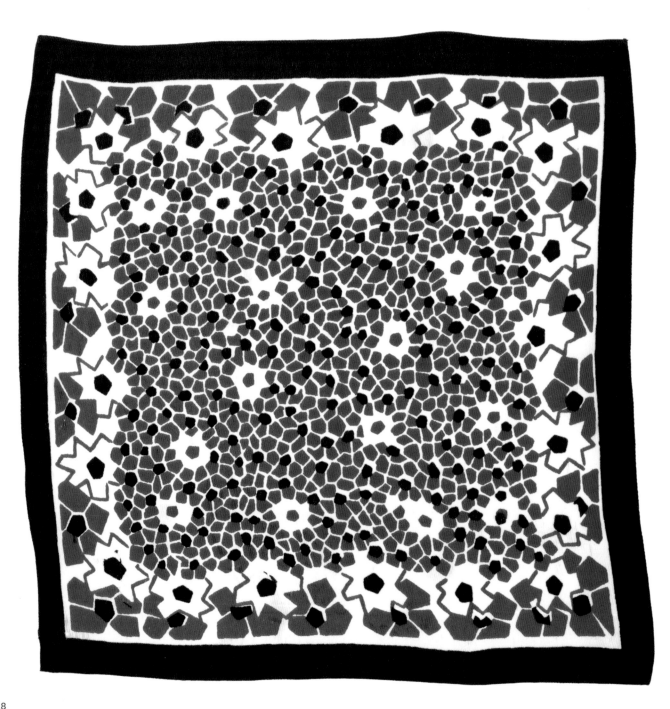

148

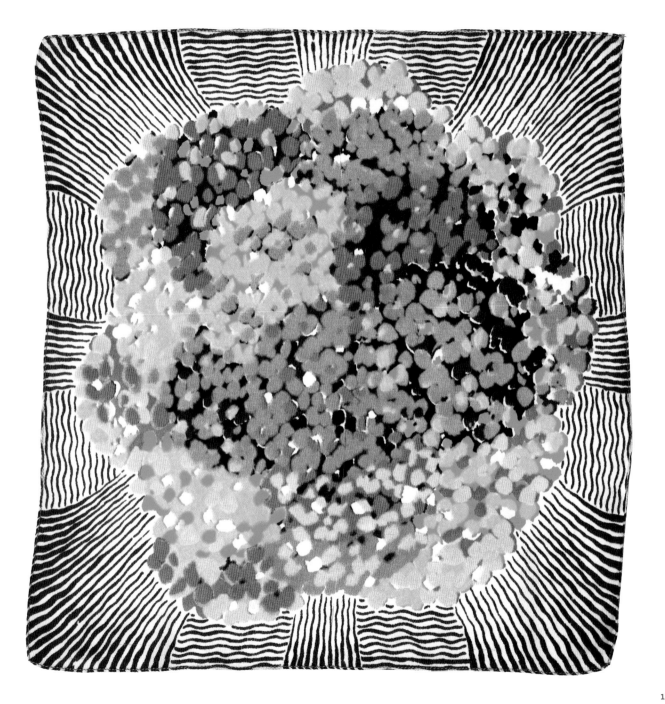

149

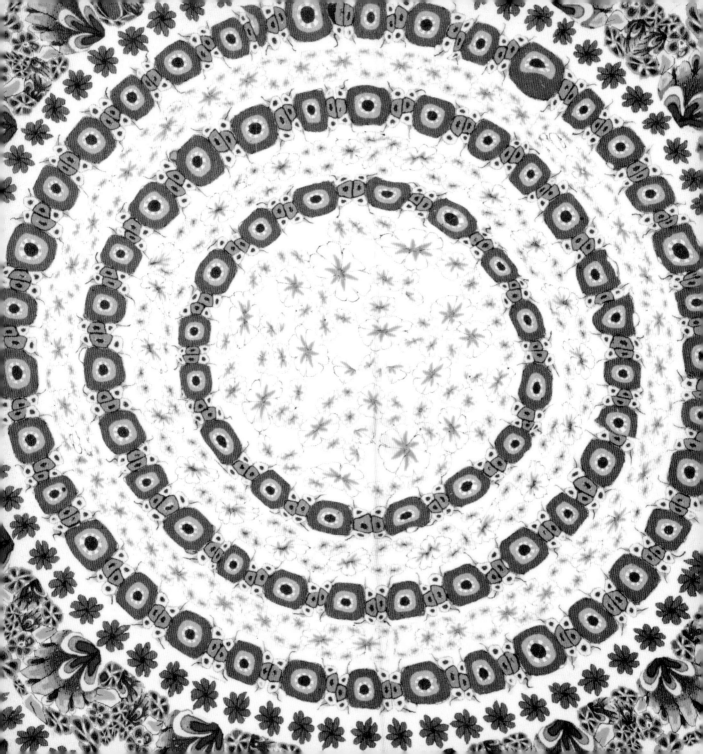

I adore that pink!

It's the navy blue of India!

DIANA VREELAND

153

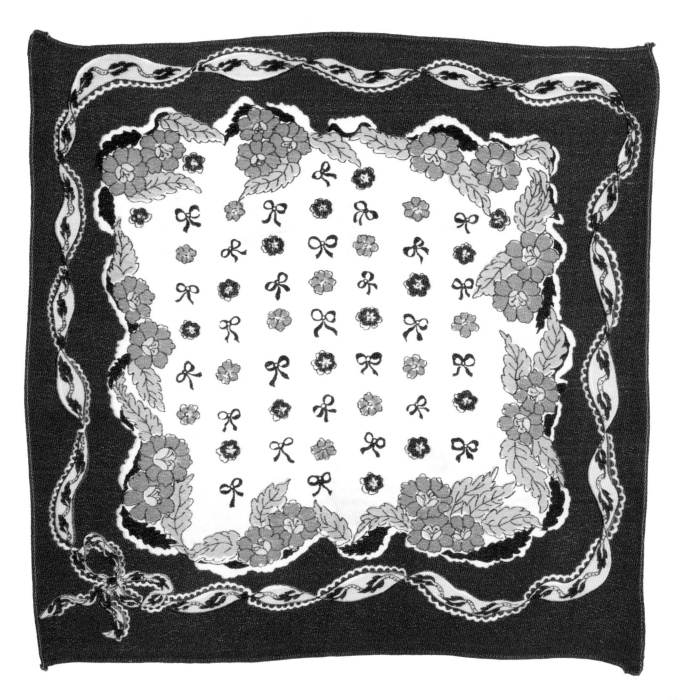

155

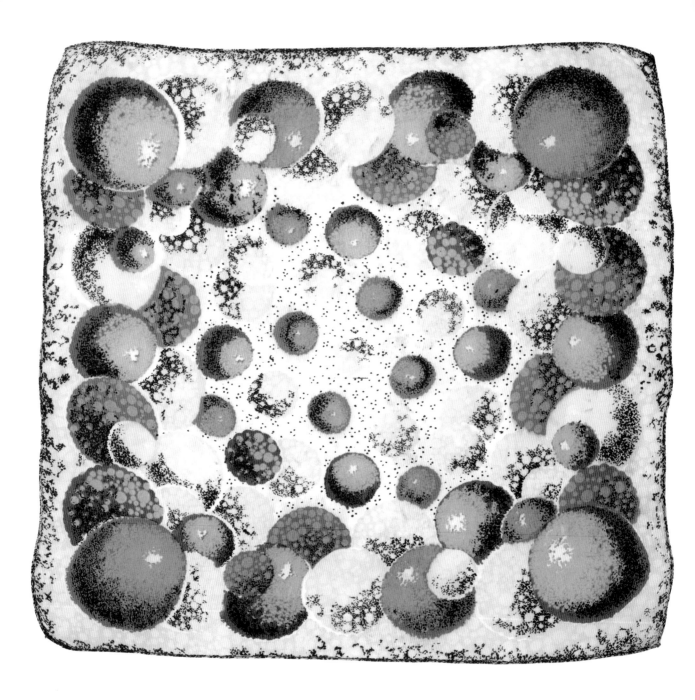

157

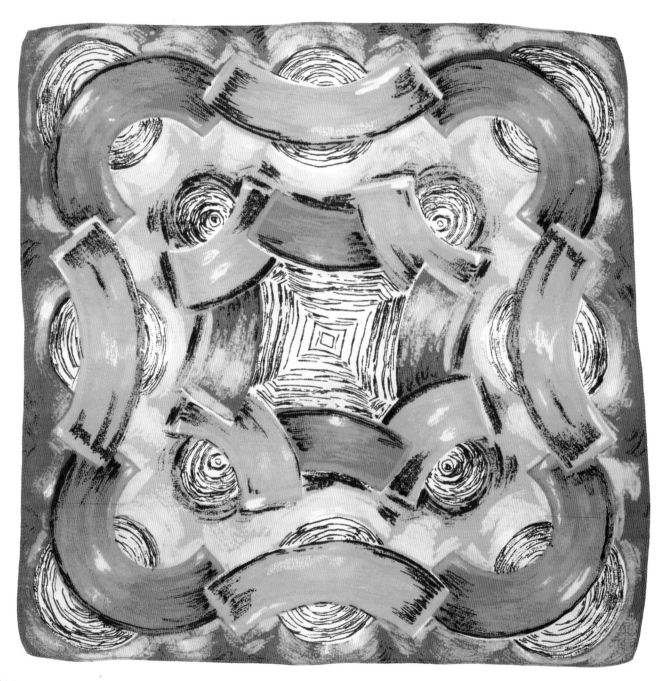

161

163

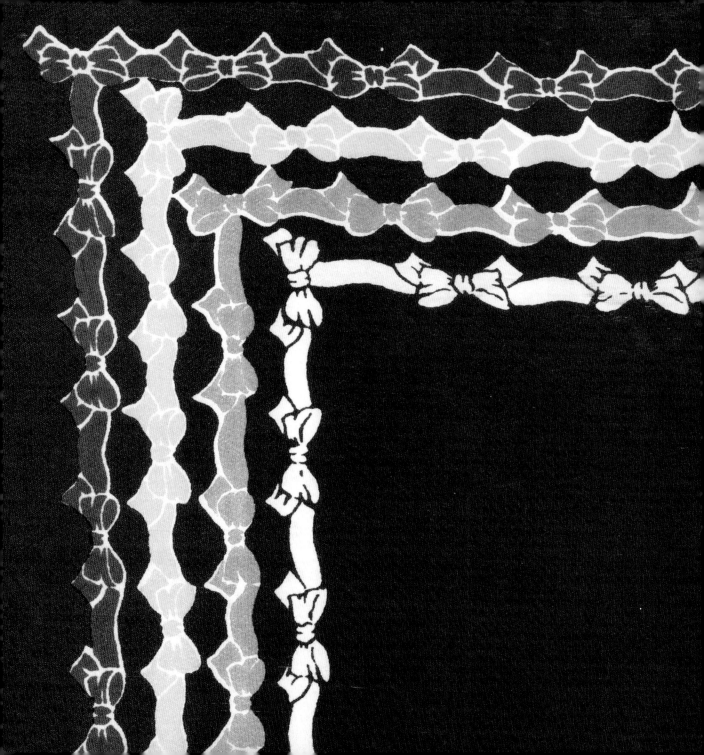

Mauve? Mauve is just pink

trying to be purple.

JAMES ABBOTT McNEILL WHISTLER

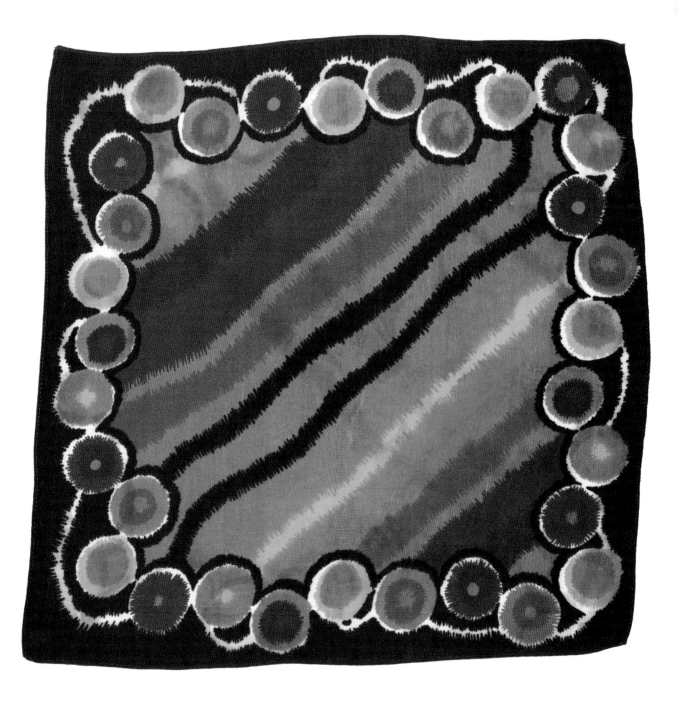

175

187

190

Warm colours are my favourites: beige, tan, brown with the addition of some cool colour for relief.

TAMMIS KEEFE

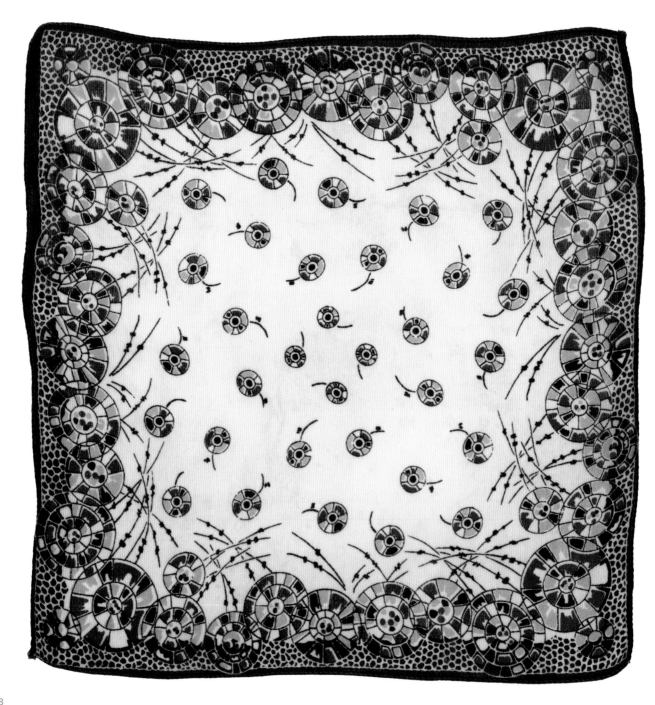

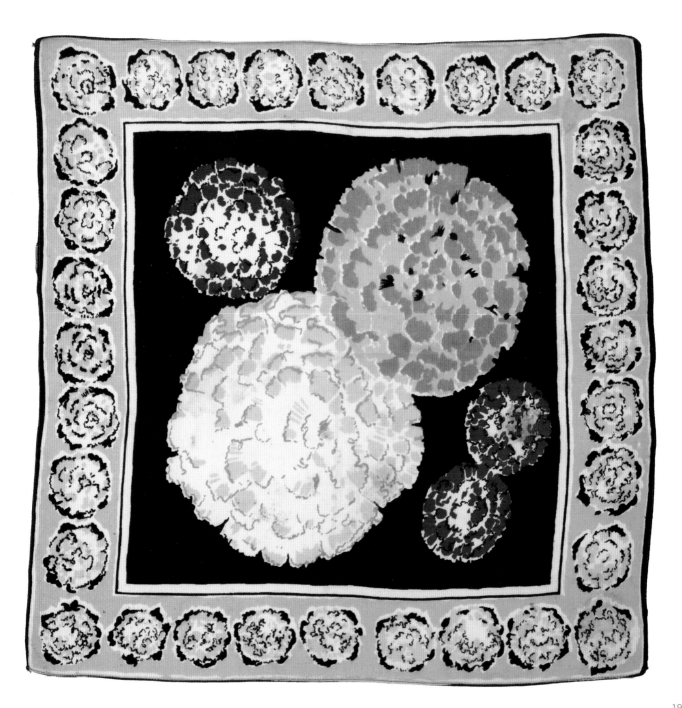

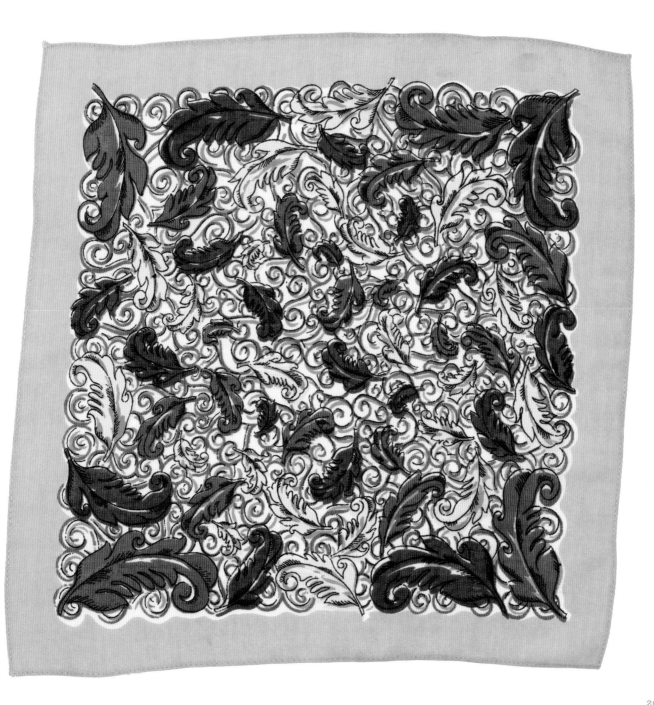

201

205

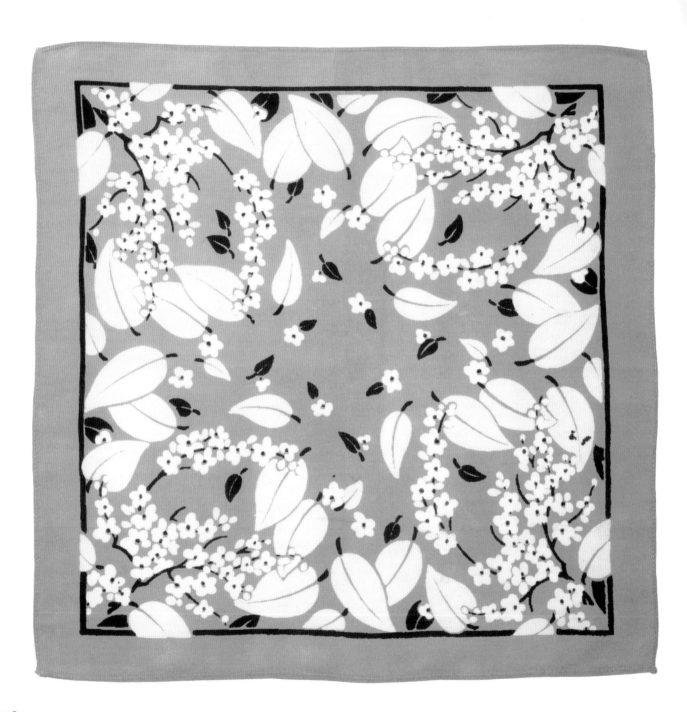

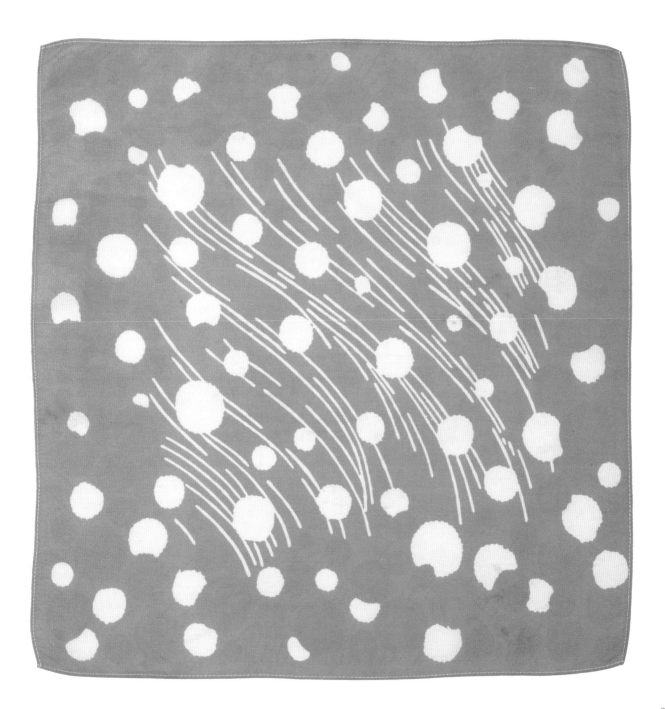

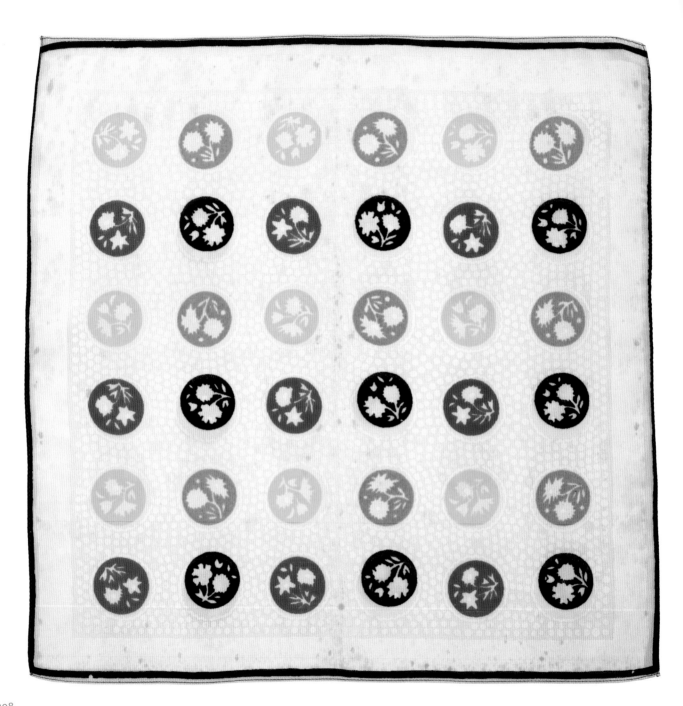

I cannot pretend to feel
impartial about colours.
I rejoice with the brilliant
ones and am genuinely sorry
for the poor browns.

WINSTON CHURCHILL

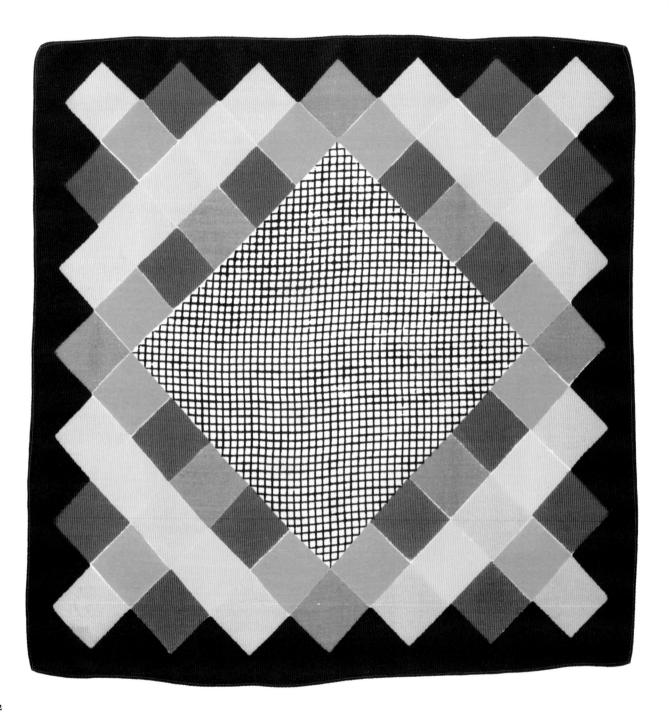

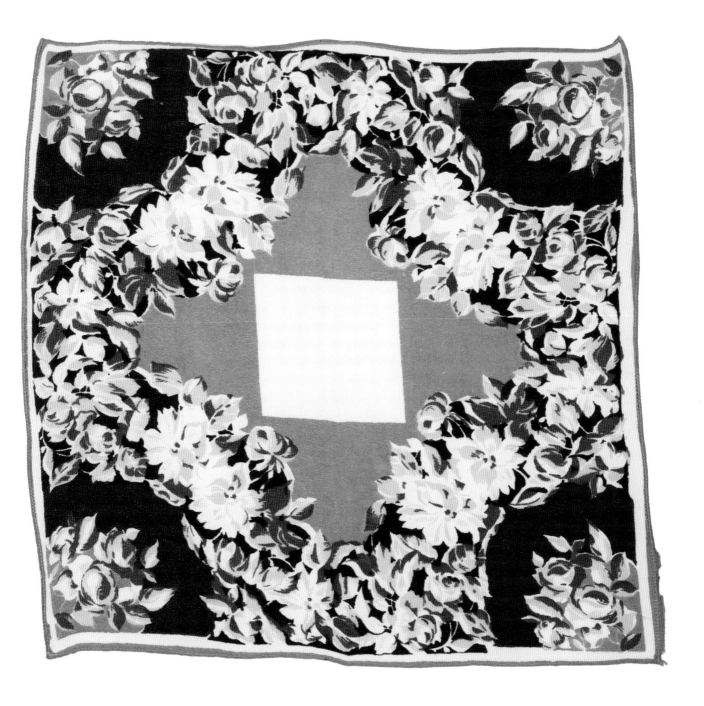

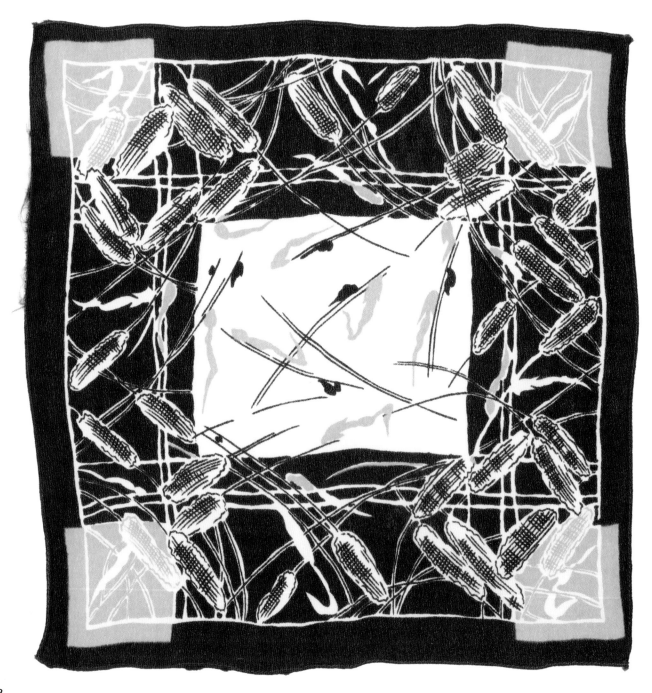

223

225

Women think of all colours
except the absence of colour.
I have said that black has
it all. White too. Their beauty
is absolute. It is the
perfect harmony.

COCO CHANEL

233

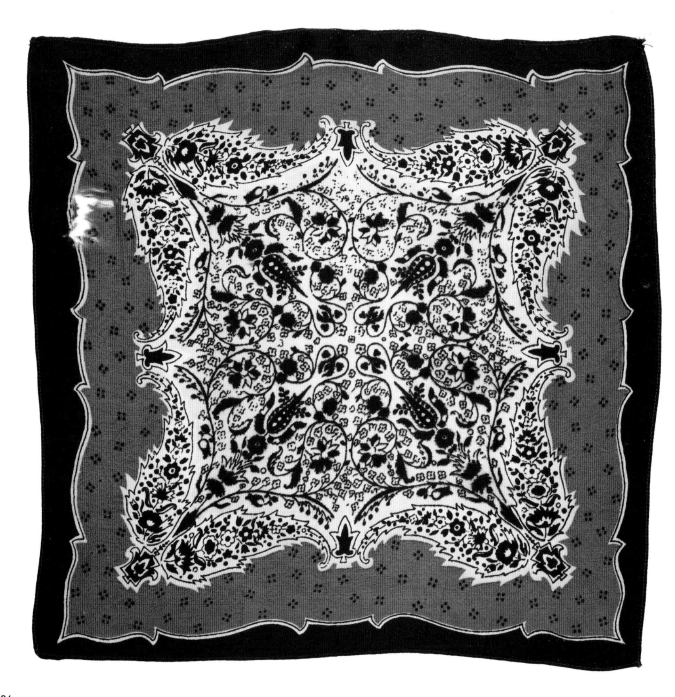

234

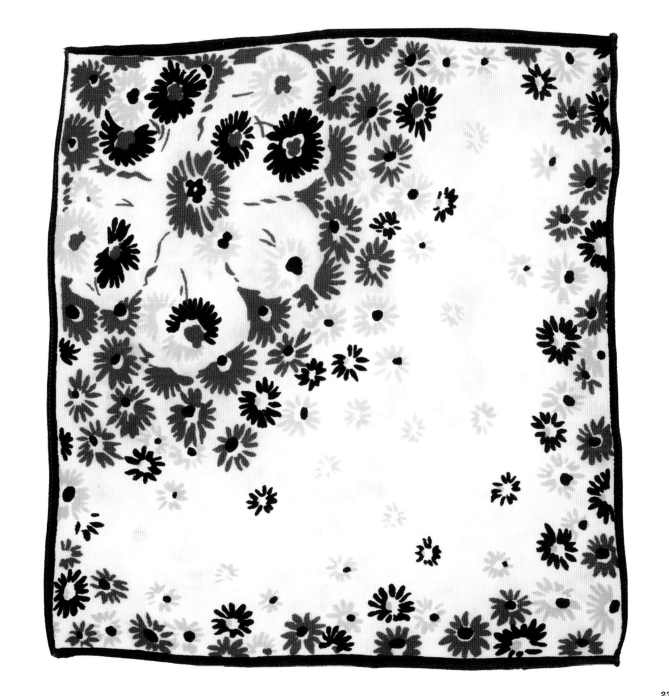

237

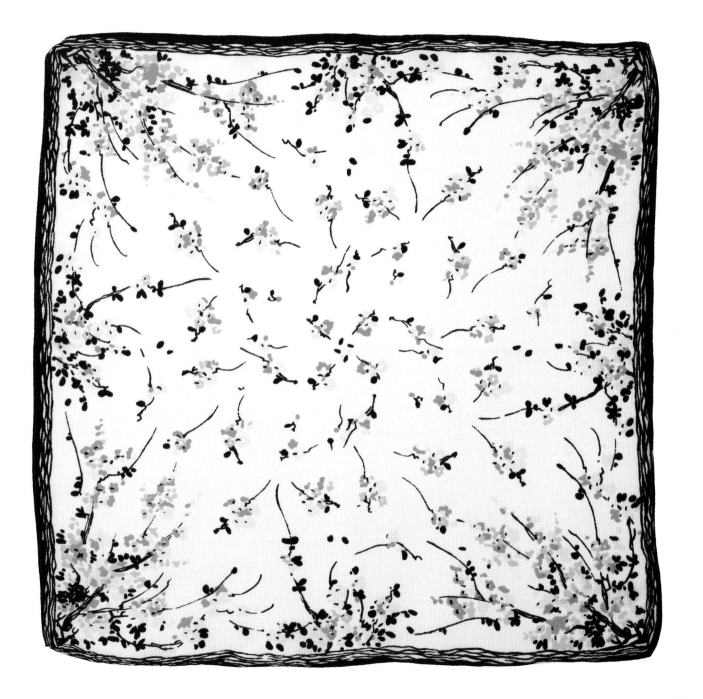

239

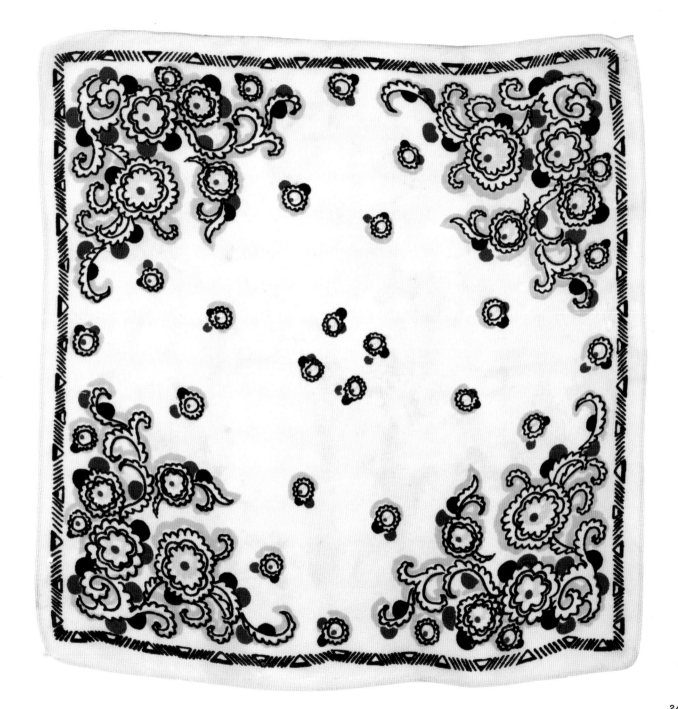

241

243

CHARACTERISTICS OF THE DECADES

1920s

Colours: Two-colour contrasts such as red and blue, brown and orange, and black and white, often outlined in black; soft, dusty pastels such as shell pinks, blues and browns with grey overtones

Motifs: Stylized angular and soft full-blown florals, complex geometric patterns, bold curves, sunbursts, sunrays, chevrons, diagonals

Influences: Art Nouveau, Art Deco, Cubism, Constructivism, Fauvism, Futurism; aeroplanes, cars, steamships; jazz, cocktail bars; early cinema; F. Scott Fitzgerald's *The Great Gatsby*

Icons: Louise Brooks, Claudette Colbert, Gloria Swanson, Elizabeth, Duchess of York (later the Queen Mother), Gary Cooper, Rudolph Valentino

1930s

Colours: Navy blue and white, soft pinks, greens, blues, neutrals

Motifs: Small geometrics, polka dots, stripes, soft small or very large-scale florals

Influences: Surrealism, Bauhaus; British monarchy, BBC television, Hollywood, Royal Ballet; Cecil Beaton, Elsa Schiaparelli, Coco Chanel; Margaret Mitchell's *Gone with the Wind* and the film adaptation

Icons: Ginger Rogers, Marlene Dietrich, Katharine Hepburn, Duke and Duchess of Windsor, Greta Garbo, Clark Gable, Errol Flynn

 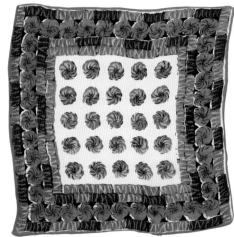

1940s

Colours: Red, white and blue; muted mustard, lilac, teal, grey, green, brown, salmon pink

Motifs: Small simple geometrics, polka dots and stripes; soft florals (small and large)

Influences: Second World War, 'Make Do and Mend'; Abstract Expressionism; swing and Glenn Miller; Christian Dior, Norman Hartnell; Daphne du Maurier, Noël Coward

Icons: Joan Crawford, Lauren Bacall, Jane Russell, Vera Lynn, Humphrey Bogart, Fred Astaire, Laurence Olivier

1950s

Colours: Contrasts of salmon pink and black, red and black, baby pink and blue; bright yellow, orange, green, lipstick pink

Motifs: Florals including roses and single-stem rosebuds, stylized graphics, illustrative motifs

Influences: Pop Art; boutique shopping; rock and roll; Givenchy, Balmain, Balenciaga; Festival of Britain, Coronation of Elizabeth II

Icons: Marilyn Monroe, Sophia Loren, Audrey Hepburn, Grace Kelly, Elvis Presley, Marlon Brando

WHERE TO FIND HANDKERCHIEFS

Collecting vintage handkerchiefs is relatively inexpensive and can be hugely rewarding. You will find them in all sorts of unusual places. In general, vintage clothing shops are not the best place to start your search as they tend not to stock handkerchiefs. Vintage fashion fairs offer a far greater choice and have become very popular, with new venues opening all the time. Details of these and other, more general fairs can be found on the internet and in local papers.

Although they offer a fairly limited assortment of vintage garments, antique fairs can also be a good place to look. You may happen upon a neglected handkerchief tucked away in a case, a chocolate box, a biscuit tin or even a bible. Handkerchiefs are not always displayed, so it is definitely worth asking dealers whether they have any in stock. If you are an avid collector, it is a good idea to get to know dealers who regularly handle handkerchiefs as they may source them on your behalf.

Like antique fairs, general auction houses will often have an assortment of handkerchiefs that have been found unexpectedly in a chest of drawers or an unlikely tea tin. Unfortunately they are often grouped with assorted haberdashery or linens in a single lot, which can prove costly. If you have a friend with a shared passion for vintage textiles, you could bid together on grouped items and then split the lot between you.

Flea markets, yard sales, *brocantes* (French bric-a-brac sales) and what are called in the UK car boot sales are also rich hunting grounds. Online auction sites such as eBay are a particularly good source of American handkerchiefs.

VINTAGE FASHION FAIRS

UK

Battersea Vintage Fashion Fair (London): *vintagefashionfairs.com*

Blind Lemon Vintage (Bath, Bristol, Cardiff, Cheltenham, Gloucester, Hungerford and Swansea): *blindlemonvintage.co.uk*

Clerkenwell Vintage Fashion Fair (London): *clerkenwellvintagefashionfair.co.uk*

Decorative Fairs (Chester, Liverpool, Manchester and Wilmslow): *decorativefairs.co.uk*

Frock Me! (London and Brighton): *frockmevintagefashion.com*

The London Vintage Fashion Fair (London): *pa-antiques.co.uk*

Time After Time (shops in Stroud and Gloucester): *stroudvintage.com*

Vintage Vogue: The Essex Vintage Fashion Fair (Brentwood): *essexvintagefashionfair.com*

USA

Manhattan Vintage Clothing Show (New York City): *manhattanvintage.com*

Vintage Fashion Expo (Santa Monica and San Francisco, CA): *vintageexpo.com*

Vintage Fashion and Textile Show (Sturbridge, MA): *vintagefashionandtextileshow.com*

Australia

Vanity Fair Markets (Sydney): *vanityfairmarkets.com*

ANTIQUE FAIRS

The best way to find antique fairs in your area is by searching online or looking through local papers. Antique fairs are so widespread that it is impossible to list them all. However, the following links should offer some useful suggestions.

UK

Adams Antiques Fairs (event organizer): *adamsantiquesfairs.com*

Antiques News & Fairs (online newspaper): *antiquesnews.co.uk*

BADA (The British Antique Dealers' Association): *bada.org*

Homes & Antiques (magazine of the *Antiques Roadshow*): *homesandantiques.com*

International Antiques & Collectors Fairs (event organizer): *iacf.co.uk*

LAPADA (The Association of Art & Antiques Dealers): *lapada.org*

P&A Fairs (event organizer): *pa-antiques.co.uk*

Take Five Fairs (Woking, Brighton and Twickenham): *antiquefairs.co.uk*

USA

The American Antiques Show (New York City): *theamericanantiquesshow.org*

Antique Dealers' Association of America: *adadealers.com*

California Country Antique Show (Los Altos, CA): *californiacountryshow.com*

The Magazine Antiques: *themagazineantiques.com*

Rhinebeck Antiques Fair (Rhinebeck, NY): *rhinebeckantiquesfair.com*

AUCTION HOUSES AND SITES

eBay: *ebay.com*

Etsy: *etsy.com*

Kerry Taylor Auctions (London): *kerrytaylorauctions.com*

Rosebery's (London): *roseberys.co.uk*

Ruby Lane: *rubylane.com*

MARKETS

Please check the websites below for up-to-date opening times. Vintage collectibles are generally only sold on certain days, as indicated.

UK

Brick Lane Market (London): *visitbricklane.org* Sunday mornings

Camden Market (London): *camden-market.org* Primarily weekends

Covent Garden Market (London): *coventgardenlondonuk.com* Monday mornings

Portobello Market (London): *portobellomarket.org* Fridays and Saturdays

Spitalfields Market (London): *spitalfields.co.uk / oldspitalfieldsmarket.com* Thursdays

France

Les Puces de Paris (Saint-Ouen): *parispuces.com* Weekends

USA

Alameda Point Antiques Faire (Alameda, CA): *alamedapointantiquesfaire.com* First Sunday of the month

Brimfield Antique and Collectibles Show (Brimfield, MA): *brimfieldshow.com* Selected dates in May, July and September

GreenFlea Market (New York City): *greenfleamarkets.com* Sundays

Hell's Kitchen Flea Market (New York City): *hellskitchenfleamarket.com* Weekends

Long Beach Outdoor Antique and Collectible Market (Long Beach, CA): *longbeachantiquemarket.com* Third Sunday of the month

Rose Bowl Flea Market (Pasadena, CA): *rosebowlstadium.com* Second Sunday of the month

Scott Antique Markets (Atlanta, GA, and Ohio): *scottantiquemarket.com* Second weekend of the month

3rd Sunday Market (Bloomington, IL): *thirdsundaymarket.com* Third Sunday of the month, May–October

Informal sales are often advertised in local papers or on community websites.

MUSEUMS

UK

Fashion Museum and Assembly Rooms (Bath): *museumofcostume.co.uk*

The Hunterian Museum and Art Gallery (Glasgow): *hunterian.gla.ac.uk*

Macclesfield Silk Museums (Macclesfield): *silkmacclesfield.org.uk*

Museum of London (London): *museumoflondon.org.uk*

Victoria & Albert Museum (London): *vam.ac.uk*

The Whitworth Art Gallery (Manchester): *whitworth.manchester.ac.uk*

USA

The Costume Institute at the Metropolitan Museum of Art (New York City): *metmuseum.org/works_of_art/the_costume_institute*

Australia

Powerhouse Museum (Ultimo): *powerhousemuseum.com*

Le Miroir des Modes, no. 8, August 1927. The cover of a 1920s fashion magazine illustrates the popular fashion for the handkerchief hemline, an uneven hem that resembled the soft points of a handkerchief. This feature became fashionable again during the 1970s.

CONSERVATION, STORAGE AND ALTERNATIVE USES

In the 1940s a public health campaign was launched in Britain advocating the use of the handkerchief with the tagline: 'Coughs and sneezes spread diseases: trap the germs in your handkerchief.' Handkerchiefs were designed to be used, and were boiled with a drop of disinfectant in the weekly wash to remove all germs. Most of the handkerchiefs in this book were made before the electric washing machine became commonplace, and would have been rigorously washed and scrubbed by hand, and then perhaps starched.

Washing by hand remains the safest way to clean vintage handkerchiefs, although most are fairly robust. Examples from the 1940s and 1950s, which were produced mainly in silk, cotton or rayon, are unlikely to run or shrink in warm water, but a cool hand wash is advisable for vibrant designs. As a general rule, the brighter the dye, the more likely it is to bleed. Earlier chiffon and silk handkerchiefs from the 1920s and 1930s need to be treated with greater care, so they should either be dry-cleaned or hand-washed in cold water. Dry the handkerchief flat to prevent it from becoming misshapen.

STAIN REMOVAL

Be careful when buying a vintage handkerchief that still bears its original shop or manufacturer's sticker. Although this indicates that the handkerchief has never been used, the glue from the sticker often leaves a mark that is very difficult to remove.

Lipstick and make-up are the most common handkerchief stains. They do not wash out easily because early make-up had a heavy oil base and used strong colour pigments. Isopropyl alcohol or rubbing alcohol is effective on these types of stains. Isopropyl alcohol can be difficult to get hold of in the UK, but pharmacies may order it in for you, or you may find it easier to search online. Dab the affected area with the alcohol on a clean white cloth, but be careful not to rub it too hard. Follow by washing the handkerchief in tepid water using a colourless washing-up (dishwashing) liquid. Do not use washing-up liquid that is bright green or yellow, as it can leave a stain of its own.

Regular, colourless hairspray can work on some oil-based stains. Spray the area, leave it for a few minutes, then wipe the spray away before washing by hand.

The hardest stains to remove are 'age spots', the small brown marks that are often seen on antique fabrics. They have various causes, from damp and mildew to mites.

Both lemon juice and bicarbonate of soda are natural bleaching agents that can be used to remove stains and are activated when placed in direct sunlight. Simply squeeze a small amount of fresh or bottled lemon juice, or mix a teaspoon of bicarbonate of soda with water until it is a smooth paste, and cover the mark, leaving the handkerchief in the sun for an hour. However, sunlight can fade vintage colours and works surprisingly quickly, so it is essential to keep a close eye on your handkerchief during the stain-removal process.

Hydrogen peroxide, a chemical bleaching agent that is available at some pharmacies, can also be used to remove stains and reduce age spots. Dilute with two thirds of warm water in a colourless plastic measuring jug or similar container, and immerse the handkerchief, leaving it for several hours. Regularly inspect the colours of the print to check for fading.

Brown spots, stains, pin holes and general flaws are quite common. They are the marks of age and should not detract from the beauty of a design. Like antique wood or worn leather, the marks, darns and thinning of vintage fabrics can be appealing, adding to their history and charm.

STORAGE

Storing vintage handkerchiefs is easy because they are small. Antique fabrics should always be laid flat, as creases caused from folding them over a long period tend to become permanent.

Lie handkerchiefs flat between acid-free tissue paper in a dark storage area such as a drawer or a box. Store them with mothballs or the natural equivalents such as dried lavender, eucalyptus or cedar chips. Never use plastic bags for storing handkerchiefs as these can trap moisture.

DISPLAY

The value of vintage handkerchiefs varies a great deal. At the high end of the market it is largely dependent on who the designer is, assuming he or she can be identified, and whether the piece

Whether tied to a handbag (*above*) or adapted for display or cushions (*overleaf*), vintage handkerchiefs can be used to embellish all sorts of articles and settings to great effect.

is of particular historical interest. However, the vast majority of handkerchiefs are sold purely for their aesthetic qualities and can be bought for very little money. This gives the collector the freedom to gather and experiment with different styles and colour combinations, or to use the handkerchiefs in creative projects without having to worry about value.

A visit to a good craft fair or a stylish vintage interiors shop can be inspirational in devising new ways to use and exhibit a handkerchief collection. Collections of vintage handkerchiefs can be used to create all sorts of items, including quilts, cushions and curtains.

Picture framing is an attractive way both to display and store fabrics. Handkerchiefs can be framed inexpensively using the following method: a soft, undyed piece of cloth is stretched over the backing board of a picture frame, secured in place with a staple gun or strong masking tape, and the handkerchief is then lightly tacked around the edge to the underfabric. UV glass can be used, but is not necessary if the frame is hung out of direct sunlight. Careful consideration must be given to the placement of a framed piece as antique fabrics can fade in natural light; indeed, museums regularly rotate their exhibits to limit exposure.

Consider the colours and styles of the handkerchiefs when you are deciding which designs to frame. Selecting two colours, create a colour theme that makes a bold statement yet complements the existing scheme in a room. Similarly, grouping a design style – for example, delicate florals or strong geometrics – can enhance the overall look of a room. Frames detract from the handkerchiefs if they are too decorative, so keep to neutral shades that harmonize with the dominant colours of the group.

Individual and customized cushions are sold in many interior design shops, and many of the larger-format vintage handkerchiefs are ideal for this purpose. Use two coordinating prints of the same size, or a plain fabric in a complementary colour for the back of the cushion. Mixing a vintage handkerchief cushion with a group of plain ones shows off the design and makes it stand out from the others.

There are many ways to use vintage handkerchiefs that require a little more sewing skill. The traditional craft of quilting is perhaps the best example. Vintage handkerchiefs are the perfect size for quilts, but it is essential to make sure you have a good selection of suitable designs before embarking on such an ambitious project.

Several companies use vintage handkerchiefs for wedding invitations, although collecting a sufficient number of examples with pale backgrounds or central blank spaces (so that the printed information is legible) is potentially problematic. Using a beautiful handkerchief collection to enliven table decoration at a formal dinner can also work well, particularly if there is a unified colour scheme. Dipping the squares in liquid starch stiffens them so that they can be used as place settings. A spray starch can be used but it is difficult to get a fine, even spray, and large blobs of starch may leave a permanent yellow stain on vintage fabrics. If you are concerned about food stains, then the handkerchief can be laid under a clear square of glass or plastic that has been cut to size.

Finally, a favourite design can be displayed by tying it to the strap of a handbag or knotting it on the wrist as a bracelet or watchstrap. Of course, you can always take the traditional route of wearing it around the neck or tucked in a breast pocket, looks that were worn when the handkerchief was at the height of its popularity.

HANDKERCHIEF FABRICS AND FINISHING

FABRICS

The following types of fabric were used in the manufacturing of vintage handkerchiefs.

Cotton
A natural fabric most commonly found in pre-twentieth-century and 1950s handkerchiefs.

Nylon
A very lightweight and sheer fabric seldom used for handkerchiefs. Seen mostly in 'dress' examples of the early 1950s, with a floral print.

Rayon
A fabric made from regenerated cellulose fibre. First invented in the late nineteenth century, it was used sporadically throughout the early twentieth century but is most common in handkerchiefs of the 1940s (it was a substitute for silk during the Second World War). A rayon handkerchief may have either a sheen or matt finish and has a nice weight without being too heavy.

Silk Chiffon
A very lightweight, sheer and soft fabric. Many 1920s and 1930s handkerchiefs were handmade from floral or patterned silk chiffon.

Silk Crêpe
A light and thin fabric with a wrinkled surface and a gauzy texture. Although uncommon, some 1930s and 1940s handkerchiefs were made from silk crêpe.

Silk Twill
A superior, heavyweight fabric, rarely seen in handkerchiefs before the 1950s. The twill weave gives the surface of the silk an appealing texture of fine, diagonal lines. This kind of silk is primarily seen in haute couture.

FINISHING

Most early twentieth-century handkerchiefs are machine-edged regardless of whether they were manufactured or handmade. Unlike scarves, however, machine edging is not necessarily a sign of inferiority. Some handkerchiefs are handrolled at the hem.

BIBLIOGRAPHY

Albrechtsen, Nicky, and Fola Solanke, *Scarves*. London and New York: Thames & Hudson, 2011

Baxter-Wright, Emma, Karen Clarkson, Sarah Kennedy and Kate Mulvey, with a foreword by Zandra Rhodes, *Vintage Fashion: Collecting and Wearing Designer Classics*. London: Carlton, 2006

Erb, Phoebe Ann, *Floral Designs from Traditional Printed Handkerchiefs*. Gilsum (NH): Stemmer House, 1998

Flusser, Alan, *Clothes and the Man: The Principles of Fine Men's Dress*. New York: Villard, 1985

Gustafson, Helen, *Hanky Panky: An Intimate History of the Handkerchief*. Berkeley (CA): Ten Speed Press, 2002

Hunterian Museum and Art Gallery, Glasgow: *hunterian.gla.ac.uk*

Mendes, Valerie D., and Frances M. Hinchcliffe, *Ascher: Fabric, Art, Fashion*. London: Victoria & Albert Museum, 1987

Mihalick, Roseanna, *Collecting Handkerchiefs*. Atglen (PA): Schiffer, 2007

Murphy, J. J., *Children's Handkerchiefs: A Two Hundred Year History*. Atglen (PA): Schiffer, 1998

O'Hara, Georgina, *The Encyclopaedia of Fashion: from 1840 to the 1980s*. London: Thames & Hudson, 1986

Rhodes, Erin, 'Then and Now: The Handkerchief', *Pittsburgh City Paper*, 29 August 2001

Roe, Margaret, 'A Brief History of the Handkerchief in Europe during the Late Middle Ages through the Renaissance', *margaretroedesigns.com/ handkerchiefhist.html*

Victoria & Albert Museum Textiles and Fashion Collection, London: *vam.ac.uk*

Vogue cover archive: *vogue.co.uk*

Wilson, Betty, *Printed and Lace Handkerchiefs: Interpreting a Popular 20th Century Collectible*. Atglen (PA): Schiffer, 2003

PICTURE CREDITS

p. 7: *top left* © John Springer Collection/CORBIS; *bottom left* © Douglas Kirkland/CORBIS; *right* © CinemaPhoto/CORBIS

p. 8: © RA/Tal/Lebrecht Music & Arts

p. 12: *left* © Bettmann/CORBIS; *right* © Bettmann/CORBIS

p. 23: *above* © Everett Collection/Rex Features; *below* © MGM/RGA

ACKNOWLEDGMENTS

Special thanks to Lauren Campbell for her creative input and design solutions.

The author would also like to thank:

Gillian Horsup for allowing many handkerchiefs to be photographed from her fantastic private collection, housed in Grays Mews Antique Market, London.

Sharon Selzer for her continued support and loan of handkerchiefs from her shop, The Shop, in Brick Lane, London.

Drew Gardner and Lucinda Marland for their superb photography and all the post-production work that we never see.

My family for their support and patience.

Everyone involved at Thames & Hudson for their support in this project.

Bags kindly lent by Lie Down I Think I Love You in Amwell Street, London, a company that sells a vintage scarf or handkerchief with each of its handmade bags. *liedownithinkiloveyou.com*

Vintage tweed gentleman's jacket and brogues lent by Levisons in Brick Lane, London.

Justin Pratt at Knoll Studio for supplying the image of the Handkerchief Chair.

In memory of my father, Michael Albrechtsen, who always wore a cotton handkerchief.

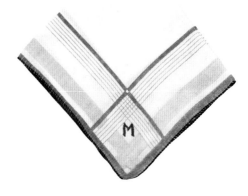

Nicky Albrechtsen is a costume designer and stylist who trained in
textile design. Her resource studio, Vintage Labels, supplies vintage
fashion and everything it encompasses to fashion studios and design
professionals seeking inspiration from period textiles and clothing.
The collection includes garments selected for their print designs,
knitwear, beadwork and silhouette. *vintagelabels.co.uk*

First published in the United Kingdom in 2012 by Thames & Hudson Ltd,
181A High Holborn, London WC1V 7QX

The Printed Square: Vintage Handkerchief Patterns for Fashion and Design
Copyright © 2012 Thames & Hudson Ltd, London
Text copyright © 2012 Nicky Albrechtsen
All photographs of individual handkerchiefs by Drew Gardner

British Library Cataloguing-in-Publication Data
A catalogue record for this book is available from the British Library

ISBN 978-0-500-51609-6

Printed and bound in China by C&C Offset Printing Co., Ltd

To find out about all our publications, please visit **www.thamesandhudson.com**.
There you can subscribe to our e-newsletter, browse or download our current
catalogue, and buy any titles that are in print.